UNIVERSITY LIBRARY
UW-STEVENS POINT

W9-BII-845

GOVERNING

METROPOLITAN AREAS

Governing
Metropolitan
Areas

A Critical Review of
Council of Governments
and the Federal Role

Melvin B. Mogulof
THE URBAN INSTITUTE
WASHINGTON, D. C.

Copyright © 1971 by

The Urban Institute
2100 M Street, N.W., Washington, D.C. 20037

ISBN 87766-021-2
Library of Congress Catalog Card No. 76-186305
UI 107-19

December 1971

The research for this study was supported by a grant from the Department of Housing and Urban Development. All views expressed are those of the author, and do not necessarily reflect approval or endorsement of the Department of Housing and Urban Development or The Urban Institute.

Refer to URI- 70004 When Ordering.

Available from:

Publications Office
The Urban Institute
2100 M Street, N.W.
Washington, D.C. 20037

List price: $2.25

Printed in the United States

B /73 /3**M**

JS
422
.M64

ACKNOWLEDGMENTS

Financial support for the work reported here was provided by the Department of Housing and Urban Development through its support of the Urban Governance Program at The Urban Institute.

The following persons were good enough to read and comment on all or portions of a draft copy of this report: Joseph H. Lewis, Francis Fisher, William Brussat, David Walker, Raymond Remy, Nicholas Thomas, Walter Scheiber, Robert Jorvig, Judson James, Marvin Hill, Frederick McLaughlin Jr., and Stephen Weitz. In many cases these comments led to revisions, but the author is of course responsible for the contents of this report. His opinions expressed here do not necessarily represent the views of The Urban Institute or its sponsors.

Melvin B. Mogulof
The Urban Institute
December 1971

245693

PREFACE

The intertwining problems of the cities sometimes defy description, much less solution. In either effort, we relate more readily to yesterday's dimension of the problem and only rarely focus on emerging problems. While most energies and resources are focused on trying to alleviate problems in full flower, an occasional burst of attention is directed toward tomorrow's opportunities and tomorrow's problems. This book describes and evaluates one such burst.

Local governments suffer from multiple, overlapping jurisdictions, bureaucratic proliferation, and wasteful duplication of local-regional-state-federal agencies, each presumably designed to resolve the same problem but competing for increasingly hard-to-get public funds. Some argue that this duplication of effort and overlapping authority are in themselves "causes"—or at least serious symptoms—of urban ills.

Councils of Governments (COGs) have been created as one effort to span areawide-metropolitan problems and better serve regional intersts. Proponents of some areawide-metropolitan planning devices see them as vehicles for reducing costly duplication, stemming the economic and racial disparities between central cities and the suburbs, and coordinating the energies and resources of numerous governmental agencies.

Although much has been hoped for through these broader approaches, little evidence of performance is yet on the record. These hopes and hypotheses need a significant amount of testing and evaluation before they can be validated.

The underlying questions are critically important. Can structural change itself really cause the resources and costs of governing metropolitan areas to be reallocated differently? Will the social service functions in the cities be performed differently, in ways that really matter? Or will local aggregations of political interests continue to dominate?

The federal government has entered the metro-planning picture as a result of several requirements which demand that some regional body below the state level, yet above the city, serve as a clearinghouse for certain federal funds entering the area. A prime component in this process is OMB (Office of Management and Budget) Regulation A-95 which established requirements and guidelines for federal planning grants being made available to metropolitan areas. The effects of A-95 are described in this study.

Designating a COG as a clearinghouse gives that body, in principle, the opportunity and obligation to review and comment on every application for federal funds—and plans to spend them—submitted by any of COG's member bodies. These funds cover a wide range of physical and social needs. The planning grants are intended to provide money for staffs to work independently of individual local governments so that regional reviews will be able to modify local actions in the interests of all in the metropolitan area.

Does the clearinghouse planning grant scheme work? How? What, specifically, do particular federal agencies have to do to insure its working? What happens to COGs as a consequence? These are some of the specific questions this book probes as a result of the direct field observations undertaken by the author.

The subject of this book and its author have been pursuing each other for some time. The opportunity for capture resulted when the Urban Governance Program at The Urban Institute and Melvin Mogulof, one of our senior research staff, joined forces to raise some questions needing solid emperical answers based on field observation.

William Gorham, President
The Urban Institute

Washington, D. C.
December 1971

CONTENTS

I. INTRODUCTION

A feature story in the *New York Times* (April 19, 1970) reported:

> While the Federal system of the United States has been undergoing severe strain in recent years, an important new level of government has sprung up almost unnoticed by the public. More than 140 Councils of Government—voluntary organizations of municipalities and counties—have been established across the country to attack areawide problems.

The national office serving Councils of Governments (and other regional councils) issued figures in May 1970 which indicated the growth of Councils of Government (COGs) to be even more dramatic than described in the *New York Times* story. Between 1968 and 1969 the National Service to Regional Councils reported that COGs (defined as councils of governing bodies containing a majority of locally elected officials) grew from 100 to 175 in number. By 1971 there were over 300. Further, almost every one of the nation's 247 Standard Metropolitan Statistical Areas (SMSAs) had a regional council of some type (COGs, Economic Development Districts, Regional Planning Commissions, etc.).[1]

No matter what the bias of a particular reviewer, he must admit, the *New York Times* to the contrary, that the COG is not now a "new level of government." It is a Council *of* Governments, a governmental *conference*, an *association* of governments, or any variety of other names, most of which carefully indicate that the COG is meant to be a coming together of governments on a voluntary basis, but not a government in itself.

We would suggest that the confused image of whether the COG is actually a new level of government is not entirely accidental. When faced with the real problems and need for action on a metropolitan basis it would be surprising if some COGs did not pretend to more authority

1

than they have.* In terms of their federal benefactors, it is also likely that many COGs do not mind appearing as if they are a government with the capacities of a government to act and to effect change.

The image of the COG as a new level of government is further complicated because a small number of regional councils have won (or aspire to win) limited governmental powers. The Minneapolis-St. Paul area's Metropolitan Council, for example, now has taxing authority and the power to plan and carry out antipollution measures, solid-waste disposal, zoning and noise abatement in a seven-county area. Or in the case of the Portland, Oregon metropolitan area, the membership of the COG is essentially the same as the newly enabled Metropolitan Services District which would have the power to raise taxes and implement programs on a metropolitan basis. In the San Francisco area, the COG was an initiator of an aborted legislative effort to establish regional "home rule" in the Bay Area by giving the COG the authority to carry out programs in a number of functional areas.

In addition to the small number of COGs which seem to be moving toward acquiring governmental powers, there are other COGs which have a certain capacity because of federal (and sometimes state) program funds which they administer. These grants for particular purposes make the COG an implementer (as well as planner and coordinator), and in that way further confuse the image of what a COG really is.

The truth, of course, is that the COG is no one thing. In some cases, for specific functions it acts as an agent of the federal or state government in carrying out an area-wide purpose. In other cases the COG is in the midst of efforts to move it from a voluntary association to something resembling a mechanism for limited metropolitan governance, and in still other cases new attempts at metropolitan governmental structure in areas such as Dade

---

*This report will use the terms "regional" and "metropolitan" interchangeably. Both are meant to connote a multijurisdictional area comprising contiguous urban populations.

The Federal Office of Management and Budget seems to use "metropolitan" as connoting an urban concentration while "regional" implies contiguous political jurisdictions of a generally rural character. Nicholas Thomas, formerly deputy director of HUD's Office of Planning and Development, suggests that the clearest designations would be "areawide-metropolitan" and "areawide-nonmetropolitan."

County, Nashville, Indianapolis, etc., have been mistakenly identified as COGs. It is little wonder that newspaper reporters view the COG as a "government," that COGs themselves do so (particularly when it is tactically advantageous), and that federal agencies supporting the COGs sometimes repeat the error.

It might be argued that the illusion of the COG as a government is a necessary "psychological" response to the problems of our metropolitan areas. It is possible that we look at all of those facts of urban life which do not respect the arbitrary boundary lines of our municipalities, and we proceed to invest a voluntary association of governments with the assumed capacity to do something about our metropolitan problems.

The something that needs doing concerns the planning for and expenditure of resources, as determined by the needs in a metropolitan area, where these needs seem less capable of being dealt with by the cumulative actions of individual governments in that area. At present almost all of our metropolitan areas are "logical" systems of action devoid of a central policy mechanism. In effect the subunits in a metropolitan system are dominant, and the governments of these units tend to act as if they were systems of action unto themselves. Thus individual governmental units make decisions which have great impact upon other subunits in a metropolitan system, but there has been no mechanism able to reconcile these actions to the advantage of a total metropolitan system. Obviously the COG is a start toward being such a mechanism, and its abilities and disabilities are primary subjects of this report.

The existence of a great number of potential metropolitan action systems (each of the 247 SMSAs might be considered to have such potential) marked by the dominance of city subunits has become a much greater concern in the past decade.* The flight of the white middle class as well as industry out of the central city coupled with the revenue problems of almost every core city has

---

*The concern for matching our governmental capacities with the configuration of a metropolitan population is hardly new. The creation of the City of New York out of 5 counties was early evidence of such concern, and efforts at annexation of small cities by central cities has been a long-used tactic for dealing with the problems of metropolitan governance. In recent years local resistance and new state legislation have diminished the utility of annexation moves.

highlighted the problem. One response to the problem has been the increasing and direct involvement of the federal government in providing resources to deal with the peculiar problems of central cities.

Victor Jones, a long time student of the metropolitan scene, has noted that "the most startling and far-reaching change in American federalism is the emergence of the National Government as the focus for discussion of urban and metropolitan affairs."[2] Presumably the reasons for Professor Jones' observation are his expectation that co-operative arrangements amongst local governments and the intervention of the state government would have been the most likely tactics for dealing with metropolitan problems. There is a literature which suggests that local co-operative arrangements have been extensive and at times effective. This literature draws its strength from the fact that the American voter has almost consistently defeated efforts to restructure metropolitan areas into larger units of government better approximating patterns of residence. The inference drawn is that current arrangements, despite the poor fit of local government to a metropolitan population (or perhaps the excellent fit of separate governments to the special populations into which we divide ourselves), do well enough in meeting the service needs of the majority of metropolitan voters.

If the metropolitan voter seems largely satisfied with the fragmented character of metropolitan government, and the federal government has become a powerful actor in the metropolitan area, the state government also remains an important (and potentially the most important) actor on the metropolitan scene. It is state legislation which creates a Metropolitan Council having real authority to govern in the Minneapolis-St. Paul area; and enabling legislation for Metropolitan Service Districts in Oregon; and the legislative base for "Uni-Gov" in Indianapolis-Marion County, Indiana. It is also state legislation which creates the multi-jurisdictional special-purpose agencies which in the case of the San Francisco Bay Area, and elsewhere, have become a new regional layer of fragmented special purpose government.

For those concerned about the health of America's pluralism the multiple centers of government on the metropolitan scene could be seen as encouraging. Surely they represent the potential, if not the actualization of different

4

approaches to our public life. It is these local units that Daniel Elazar must have meant when he wrote that "American federalism has been able to combine strength at the center with local control. . . ."[3] However, recent federal legislation has concerned itself with some of the costs of local control in an attempt to achieve more rational federal action in metropolitan areas. The enablement of metropolitan "clearinghouses" through the Demonstration Cities and Metropolitan Development Act of 1966 and the Intergovernmental Cooperation Act of 1968 is an important measure toward achieving a new balance between "strength at the center" and "local control." As noted, these acts have helped to stimulate the establishment of clearinghouses in almost every one of the country's SMSAs.

Section 204 of the Demonstration Cities and Metropolitan Development Act specifies that application for federal loans and grants in a variety of functional areas "shall be submitted for review to any areawide agency which is designated to perform metropolitan or regional planning for the area within which the assistance is to be used. . . ." These applications for loans or grants shall be accompanied:

> (a) by the comments and recommendations with respect to the project involved by the areawide agency . . . and
> (b) by a statement by the applicant that such comments and recommendations have been considered prior to formal submission of the applications.[4]

Title IV of the Intergovernmental Cooperation Act of 1968 includes the following statements of policy:

> The President shall . . . establish rules and regulations governing the formulation, evaluation, and review of federal programs and projects having a significant impact on area and community development. . . . All viewpoints—national, regional, state, and local—shall, to the extent possible, be fully considered and taken into account in planning federal or federally assisted development programs and projects. . . . To the maximum extent possible, consistent with national objectives, all federal aid for development purposes shall be consistent with and further the objectives of state, regional and local comprehensive planning.[5]

ᴏ ᴍᴃ

Circular A-95, dated July 24, 1969, established administrative regulations which embrace both of the above pieces of legislation. This circular sought to stimulate a "network of state, regional and metropolitan planning and development clearinghouses" to receive and disseminate information about proposed projects; to coordinate between applicants for federal assistance; to act as a liaison between federal agencies contemplating federal development projects, and to conduct an "evaluation of the state, regional or metropolitan significance of federal or federally assisted projects."[6]

As of September 1970 the National Service to Regional Councils reported that 99 percent of 192 metropolitan clearinghouses were either Councils of Government or regional planning commissions.* The large majority of these clearinghouses were established after the enactment of the 1966 and 1968 federal legislation, and there is common agreement that the spectacular growth in regional councils is in response to this legislation. In an area where local referenda and state legislation had produced almost nothing with regard to metropolitan governing mechanisms, federal legislation, coupled with the use of Department of Housing and Urban Development 701 planning funds for institutional support, has almost overnight established the potential for evolving "a new level of government."

This book details the results of an examination of seven metropolitan clearinghouses over a period of four months.** The questions we will seek to answer include: (1) How does the metropolitan clearinghouse operate? (2) What is the character of its actions? (3) What forces contribute to the taking of these actions? We also deal at length with the organizational environment of the clearinghouse and its developmental problems as well as future

---

*In the remainder of this book we shall use clearinghouse or COG as the generic terms for metropolitan mechanisms such as COGs and regional planning commissions. The regional planning commission with its tendency to have citizen "elite" leaders as policy makers may not meet our earlier definition of a "coming together of governments on a voluntary basis." But the evidence is clear that, under the impetus of HUD criteria for 701 funding and OMB's A-95 procedures, the two kinds of clearinghouses are becoming more like each other in structure with both being strongly representative of local government.

**The three COG/clearinghouses looked at most intensively were in the Sacramento area, the Puget Sound area and the San Francisco Bay area. Less intensive observation was made of the clearinghouses in the Minneapolis-St. Paul area, the Chicago area, the Jacksonville-Duval area, and the Dallas-Ft. Worth area.

6

prospects for metropolitan governance. We evaluate the clearinghouse process as it currently operates and speculate on the efficacy of these new metropolitan structures and processes. Efficacy for what? Originally we were occupied with the potential effectiveness of metropolitan clearinghouses in redistributing resources and that was to be our test of efficacy. The reader need not be burdened with going further to find the answer to that—none of the clearinghouses we observed were in any apparent way currently effective in the redistribution of resources. However, there are interesting clues as to future possibilities, particularly in the Minneapolis-St. Paul Council, and these will be examined further.

We reject the capacity to effect redistribution as the only (or even the most important) criteria of clearinghouse effectiveness. There are issues of effectiveness involved in the distribution (as opposed to redistribution) of public resources which are a legitimate test of the clearinghouses' utility. And put another way, it may be that the federal government through its taxing program, its cash transfers to individuals and its categorical aid programs (as opposed to the concept of revenue sharing on a population-equity basis) is the most effective redistributor, and the task of the clearinghouse is to enhance the efficiency of these federal redistributions—not to distort them.

With these last words we have opened an important problem in assessing the clearinghouse. What are the expectations held by different parties as to the proper test of clearinghouse effectiveness? If there is confusion in expectations, and there is, how do these hurt (and possibly help) the clearinghouse? In this regard we have conceived of the clearinghouse as a somewhat frail mechanism, surrounded by a series of expectations related to the way in which different forces in the environment of the clearinghouse perceive metropolitan problems. It is in this environment that the clearinghouse will have to survive by satisfying the most critical of the expectations which surround it. A more detailed look at the metropolitan scene which is the clearinghouse's grounds for survival follows.

NOTES

[1] National Service to Regional Councils, memorandum on "Regional Council Trends," May 21, 1970.

[2] Victor Jones, "Representative Local Government: From Neighborhood to Region," *Public Affairs Report*, University of California, Berkeley, April 1970.

[3] Daniel Elazar, *The American Partnership*, University of Chicago, 1962, p. 339.

[4] U.S. Government, Bureau of the Budget, *Circular A-95*, July 24, 1969, Attachment C.

[5] *Ibid.*, Attachment B.

[6] *Ibid.*, Attachment A.

II. THE METROPOLITAN SCENE

Problems in Governance

Norton Long has written,

> The future of the metropolis is the future of
> most of us. The quality of life that is lived in it
> is the quality of American life. . . . The question
> at issue is whether we have the wit, the courage,
> the good sense, and the goodwill to transform
> the 200-odd metropolitan areas in which the bulk
> of us live into responsibly self-governing com-
> munities.[1]

As noted earlier we are not without a history in our
attempts to develop organizational forms of government
to match our interdependencies in the metropolitan area.
Among these developments have been the special single-
purpose district, the amalgamation of local governments,
the annexation of unincorporated and incorporated communities into core cities, new regional responsibilities to
state agencies, regional multipurpose governing mechanisms, and voluntary governmental cooperation. All of
these organizational attempts rest in part on the premise
that we need additional governmental capacities in our
metropolitan areas to deal with those metropolitan problems which go beyond the aggregation of individual city-
county responses to problems.

In the last decade this push to consider metropolitan
forms of governance has run into a seeming counter-
tendency to further partialize our governments in metropolitan areas. This movement toward decentralization (or
noncentralization) of government of course owes much
to the interest by some minority group leadership in
bringing their areas of residence under local community
control. Some analysts have counterposed minority interest in community control to metropolitan governance.

Piven and Cloward suggested that metropolitan government, by being responsive to coalitions of suburban and inner-city whites, would frustrate the promise of urban political power to the black masses.[2]

But the argument for a two-tier form of metropolitan government (i.e., a regional unit plus local units) holds out the hope that the seemingly irreconcilable moves to fragmentation via community control and to metropolitan forms of government are in fact reconcilable.[3] The key to such an accommodation, if it is to result in two tiers of government in metropolitan areas, is some agreement as to which decisions are best determined by the smallest units of government and which demand some form of metropolitan governance.

The kinds of activities which seem to need a metropolitan decision-making capacity are: (1) those which are supportive of the jurisdictional boundary crossings which people in metropolitan areas normally engage in in great numbers (e.g., highway planning, mass transit, open space planning, airport planning and operation, planning for the regional job market, etc.) ; (2) those where the negative (or non) actions of one jurisdiction may undercut the actions of another jurisdiction (e.g., air pollution, low-cost housing, waste disposal) ; and (3) those where economies of scale may demand interjurisdictional planning and operation (e.g., water supply, specialized hospitals, etc.).[4]

This schema for determining decision areas which are metropolitan in character is hardly definitive. How many and what kinds of boundary crossings are there? Constraints on a community's action may just as likely spring from the action or inaction of the state (or federal government) as from the action of a contiguous local government. And who is to unequivocally determine at what point economy of scale makes a problem more amenable to regional rather than local (or state) action? It is likely that the answers to these questions will remain political rather than definitional. And it is just as likely that metropolitan areas will remain a profusion and confusion of governmental activity. The central idea on which we base this analysis and which underlies the federal legislation supportive of COGs, is that there are a variety of public actions in metropolitan areas which need to be rationalized (and perhaps authorized) from a metropolitan point of view. Given this assumption about the inherent metropolitan character of certain public actions, the clearinghouse through the use of Circular A-95 emerges as an institutional device with great national potential.

There are of course governmental arrangements on the metropolitan scene which predate and run parallel to the clearinghouse development. Friesema in a study of 10 cities in an SMSA found 252 interjurisdictional agreements covering many of the functional areas we have noted above.[5] In some cases the geography of a county coupled with its home rule capacities have made the county a usable vehicle for metropolitan governance. In many other cases multijurisdictional special districts have been formed, generally to perform a single function, under state enabling legislation.

An observer of the metropolitan governing scene can hardly claim that it is barren of activity. The very volume of this activity, coupled with the particular effectiveness of certain special districts (e.g., utility districts, transit districts, water commissions, etc.), has undoubtedly served to obscure from the public a sense of crisis about metropolitan governing problems. And it may help to account for the unwillingness of the voting public to agree to more powerful and "radical" metropolitan governing forms. But Walter Scheiber, director of the Metropolitan Washington COG, has made the astute observation that in creating a series of regionwide, single-purpose authorities we are actually beginning to build the very metropolitan government that many people fear, but one which is often inaccessible to the voting public. Scheiber goes on to see "the Council [COG/clearinghouse] as the only device which offers any realistic hope of developing a viable metropolitan policy process on a general basis."[6] One may not agree with Scheiber's optimism about COGs. However, their rapid expansion during the past few years, and the potential strength which has accrued to them by becoming metropolitan clearinghouses under Circular A-95, seem to make the COG/clearinghouse the most important unit of observation with regard to current issues in metropolitan governance. Their importance is underlined by the following powerful array of facts: they exist in almost all of our metropolitan areas—where other forms (such as regional planning councils) exist they are becoming like COGs; they are an evolving form with an apparent willingness to consider the problems of regional government; they are the developers (or the potential developers) of that which resembles a comprehensive approach to the way certain resources ought to be distributed in a region; and they have newly acquired influence over the expenditure of large sums of federal money (and local matching funds) in a region as the result of the A-95 process.

Before we move to a description of the clearinghouse as a structural response to the problems of regional governance, we need to be more explicit about what these problems are. First of all, our metropolitan areas have become the great centers of our population. Seventy percent of our people live in them now, and it is predicted that 85 percent of us will live in them by the year 2000. Thus the skill with which the governments of these areas deliver public resources, while enabling their citizens to feel a part of the polity, will underlay the quality of our lives.

Second, at the heart of many of our metropolitan areas lies a core city increasingly the home of aggrieved minorities, the poor and the aged. In one sense to speak of the metropolitan problem is to speak of our failures in black/brown and white relationships. And despite the small gains which have been made in residential integration, there is a likelihood that the core city of the metropolitan area will witness an increasing concentration of troubled minorities.[7] As one interviewee noted, "there are no more central city problems—only regional ones with central city implications." So long as being of color brings with it a high probability of grievance, and so long as central cities are the home of those of color, we must be wary of regional governing forms which can become devices for submerging the political will of minorities.

Third, at this time the role of the state in dealing with the problems of metropolitan governance cannot be easily predicted. State government is becoming more sophisticated; the apparent willingness of the federal government to rely on state governments in metropolitan areas is increasing; reapportionment is changing state legislatures, but perhaps not as strongly toward central cities as towards the metropolitan areas with their white, middle-class, suburban majorities.

Fourth, the problems of environmental deterioration sit particularly hard on the metropolis as a whole, and seem peculiarly demanding of metropolitan solutions.

It is against these problems and others that we need to measure the COG as a structural response.

12

COG as a Structural Response to the Problems of Regional Governance

Stanley Scott and John Bollens, two critics who write extensively about the problems of the metropolitan area, have sought to account for the popularity of the COG by noting that "it is the mildest of all approaches, building on the status quo without disturbing its formal organization. Moreover, unlike other methods, each of which produces a metropolitan government, the COG approach does not create an areawide government."[8] Scott and Bollens may not be exactly right in seeking to account for the COG's popularity by its blandness. We have previously suggested that COGs experienced their greatest growth in response to federal legislation and to the availability of 701 planning funds to COG-type agencies. Their growth was also in response to Federal Highway Administration regulations which called for areawide transportation planning in 1965 as a prerequisite to the continued flow of federal highway funds.

Bollens and Scott are of course right in attributing the extent of local governmental willingness to form COGs to the mildness of the COG approach. But it seems important to note that while the final decision for COG affiliation was a voluntary one for local government, it was largely in response to federal legislation and administrative guidelines. It is federal money, federal staff assistance and federal policy that is largely responsible for the health and/or weakness of the COG. Perhaps then there is some justice in noting that some of the most incisive comments about the weakness of the COG come from federal personnel.

The point is not to berate the federal government for the COG's current failings. It is simply to reemphasize Victor Jones' point that the federal government is a preeminent actor with regard to regional governance. In every metropolitan area, federal funds are a significant part of local public expenditures. In a few areas they may be *the* most significant part. It is entirely reasonable to expect that federal policy might require and receive strong evidence of local willingness to work through new regional forms as a prerequisite to being eligible for federal funds to deal with problems having a metropolitan impact.

What kind of a structure is the COG that the federal

13

government has nurtured into being? In describing the clearinghouse function OMB Circular A-95 uses the concepts of "coordinate," "liaison," and "evaluation of . . . metropolitan significance of federal or federally-assisted projects." The COG is to act as a point of regional intelligence to guide the federal government in its funding of a wide variety of projects contributing to the growth and development of a region. Section 204 of the Metropolitan Development Act further specifies that these review functions shall be carried out by the "agency which is designated to perform metropolitan . . . planning." The elegance of federal thinking which couples review for metropolitan significance with metropolitan planning is to be much admired. Those who wrote the law and those who drafted the implementing OMB circulars indicated that they did not want idiosyncratic reviews reflecting the *ad hoc* preferences of the reviewers but, rather, reviews within the context of an adopted regional policy plan. A good deal of the nonsense which currently passes for clearinghouse evaluation might have been saved if that early bit of wisdom had been insisted on. But the evidence is that there are many at the local as well as the federal level who are willing to settle for the appearance of a regional review process without having that process based on adopted regional policy.

The limited authority of the COG derives from the federal government. This fund of authority hardly constitutes any capacity to engage in the "painful acts of government." In a very few cases the COG (or perhaps more appropriately the clearinghouse) receives additional authority from the state legislature (as in Minneapolis-St. Paul or from the fact that the clearinghouse is a single government, essentially coterminous with the metropolitan area (as is approximated in Jacksonville-Duval County).

The policy making structure of the COG has been more influenced by HUD guidelines than by those of the A-95 circular. It is HUD funds in the 701 planning program which have become the financial support for COGs, and it is HUD guidelines which insist on the representation of a significant percentage of the metropolitan area governments on the COG's policy board. Additionally it is HUD which has begun to prod 701 planning agencies with regard to citizen participation in their policy structure. And it is HUD which has moved the COG into a new (and sometimes uncomfortable) concern

14

with social problems by requiring that a housing element be a part of the 701 agency's regional planning.

The three most important structural facts about the COG are that (1) it receives the bulk of its financial support from federal sources for the purposes of areawide planning, and these federal sources seem increasingly skeptical of planning which does not have its "payoffs" in implementation; (2) it receives its aura of authority from the A-95 circular which seems to call for a structure which can coordinate regional activities but which can also evaluate these activities against the goals articulated by regional planning; and (3) it receives its legitimacy from its member governments. But these governments do not seem to want the COG to emerge as a force different and distinct from the sum of its governmental parts. Member governments do not generally see the COG structure as an independent source of regional influence but rather as a service giver, a coordinator, a communications forum, and an insurance device for the continued flow of federal funds to local governments.

The essential structural problem for the COG is that it is being pulled in two directions: (1) to protect and serve its member governments, and (2) to make judgments and take actions which may be perceived as harmful by the COG's member governments. As a result the COG finds it extremely difficult to do things such as make critical comments about applications of member governments for federal funds, establish priorities which affect member governments, or influence local governmental actions in an attempt to make them consistent with regional planning.

It would be easy to predict great strain for an institution surrounded by deeply discordant expectations. This strain was captured in the *New York Times* report on regional councils which noted that "a common thread running through the conversations of the people who work with the Councils is that they are evolving into something different and meaningful, but no one is sure what it is."[9] Perhaps the strain is more aptly illustrated in a comment of one federal official upon reading the proposal which preceded this study. He said, "Don't come up with something which tells us they [COGs] will be better tomorrow— tell us why they are not working today."

15

This report details the evidence and apparent causes of the COGs' strain. But it must be noted that the strain in the COGs' structure is not necessarily bad. It can engender a certain excitement about the mechanism, and a fluidity which makes it an interesting organizational target for community groups seeking to maximize a point of view. In fact the reduction of the strain, through the withdrawal of any one of its provokers (i.e., agencies of the federal government or local government) might resolve the situation through the death of the mechanism. Conversely, we look to the introduction of additional strain through the emergence of the state government as an increasingly significant regional actor with its own set of expectations.

The image of the COG we mean to convey is one of a beleaguered organization, surrounded by unsure federal partners, unwilling local members and a barely awakening state government. Of course the mix and proportion of this strain is different in different areas (and how nice it would be if sophisticated federal administration could act in the light of these differentials). Some state governments, such as Texas, seem to have entered into overt and important alliances with the COG. Others such as Oregon appear to have made commitments to the establishment of a consistent regional basis for action. Neither are local governments monolithic with regard to their views of regionalism. There are individual local officials who are strong "regionalists," with local constituents who do not punish them at the ballot box for their attitudes favoring regional action. And there is a growing sentiment in metropolitan areas in support of common action and coordination (although with no agreement as to what that overworked word means). However, one repeatedly meets local officials involved with COGs who in the privacy of their office say, "tell the feds to keep the heat on—we will never be able to act together unless we are forced to."

While it would be possible to detail the differences amongst local governments with regard to their regional actions, one must finally be most impressed with their unwillingness, within the COG, to make decisions which are costly to individual member governments. Thus local governments, whatever their differences, constrain the clearinghouse to act by consensus and to plan in a way

16

which embraces the policies and plans of the constituent
local members.

Whatever the differences between local governments,
we have observed that they generally act to obtain a clearinghouse which is not costly to them. Individual leaders
may perceive that the price for this continued action by
consensus is a sense of governmental illness on the metropolitan scene. And they know that this illness will be accompanied by increasing attempts by state government to
respond with single purpose creations or the redefinition
of peculiarly metropolitan problems into fit subjects for
state agency action. Some of these actions are detailed later
in this book.

Despite the above description of problems, we see the
COGs as generally responsive to the directions inherent in
federal policy. We have already suggested that federal
policies tend to be most productive of the strain being
experienced by COGs. Difficulties in dealing with this strain
have even raised basic questions amongst COGs and federal
agencies about the continuity of federal involvement. But
despite some recurring federal ambivalence about COG
performance, the COG remains an important instrument
of federal policy at the metropolitan level.

COG as an Instrument of Federal Policy

In the Spring of 1971, the OMB issued a revision of
Circular A-95 which enormously broadened the number and
kind of federal programs subject to clearinghouse review.
We do not view this as a partisan political act by a new
administration. The predecessor circulars on which A-95
was based were issued during the Johnson Administration,
and the legislation on which the circular is based is the
product of a Democratic Congress. Nevertheless the "idea"
of A-95 seems very much in rapport with an administration
which has been experimental with regard to the decentralization of government and is generally attracted to enhancing
public administration efficiency. (We have heard A-95 rationalized as being "simply good public administration.")
Despite the *prima facie* reasons for expanding the role of
the clearinghouse, we might cautiously ask what in its past

17

successes warrants this show of federal confidence. The question becomes even more delicate when compared to Scott and Bollens' description of the COG as "the mildest of approaches," and when seen in the context of all of those federal officials who decry the performance of the COG to date.*

We do not have a single "powerful" idea to explain the expansion of A-95. But a cataloguing of a variety of ideas may provide clues as to what we have found in the federal relationship to the clearinghouse and help to explain other materials to be presented in this paper.

Perhaps the best explanation for the A-95 expansion lies in the mildness of the A-95 approach. After all, federal politics are not a thing apart from local politics. There are always costs to a national administration for actions which are seen as unpalatable by local government. The broad acceptability of the A-95 process to local governments, coupled with the look of rationality and "good public administration," make it a highly attractive device for expansion. Other reasons for expansion may be:

> (a) There is no common agreement as to what an effective clearinghouse/COG does. Those who view it as a grounds for communication, as in fact the kind of mechanism which the word clearinghouse denotes, have much to be satisfied with. The clearinghouse does clear—it lets affected governments know what is happening, and it can be highly effective in those situations where a change in proposed action benefits "B" while causing no discomfort to "A". If that is what the clearinghouse is supposed to do then there is a logical imperative to placing all federal actions having regional implications under A-95 review.

> (b) The A-95 process is not costly to the federal government. It makes the federal government look like a good regional citizen while minimally impairing federal decision-making prerogatives. In effect, federal agencies have a remark-

---

*The situation may not be unlike federal experience with the Community Action Program. The community action idea was in the process of being tested in a small number of cities by the President's Committee on Juvenile Delinquency. The experience was at best mixed when community action went nationwide under the OEO program. With A-95 clearinghouses, as with the CAP, it may be an example of the political maxim of "you go with what you've got."

ably cheap form of protection in the A-95 process. Federal agencies are now able to claim that a potential grant was checked through with all of the affected local governments. And nominally it was. In a sense A-95 co-opts local government into the federal decision-making process at a very small cost. The costs could be seen as rising in proportion to the number of instances in which a COG raised objections to a requested federal funding action. To extend the argument, one might suggest that the A-95 process could be abandoned at precisely the time at which regional "review and comment" began to seriously narrow federal latitude for action.

(c) The clearinghouse is a federal property. It is the federal entry in the field of metropolitan governance. It may be weak or ineffective, but it is the best hope on the regional scene at this time, and it ought to be given every chance for success before it is pronounced a failure. Under this conception, expanding the A-95 process may be seen as increasing the clearinghouse's chances for success.

(d) There is a model for change which argues that the best thing the federal government can do at this time is help to surface a regional point of view, and hope that, in the give and take of decision making, this regional point of view will be influential. Thus the constant push to expand the purview of A-95 on the assumption that there is benefit in exposing as many decision situations as possible to the potential impact of a regionally oriented agency.

(e) There are those in the federal government who *do* view the COG developmentally. They are not frightened by the strain and the evident weakness surrounding the COG. They are more impressed with the survival tasks that the COG as an organization has, and are prepared to settle for small payoffs now with the hope that they are creating the grounds for a genuine metropolitan capacity for governance in the future.

Inadvertently we have come back to the basic dilemma of our evaluation. What is it that one values? In looking at the COG as a potential instrument of federal policy, we

19

have tried to suggest some of the things that the federal government values. These value questions, which constitute some of the major criteria used in the development of this report, are:

>1. Does the COG serve as a forum for communication between local governments and the federal government?
>2. Are the COGs able to develop a metropolitan point of view on problems and use this point of view in assessing requests for the use of federal funds? And does this point of view influence the decisions being made by local government on problems of regional import?
>3. Is there a developmental process taking place with COGs becoming organizationally more secure and better able to fight and win on regional issues?

Parenthetically, one must ask if any or all of the above tasks are being pursued without incurring unacceptable costs to the federal government. And just who in the federal government perceives the action of a COG to be costly? Clearly, the acceptability of an action may be perceived very differently by a line department and by the OMB. In effect, the COG may emerge in the role of agent of the OMB, in trying to get line federal departments to act in certain ways. It may turn out to be more useful to see the COG not as a general instrument of federal policy, but rather as a regional instrument of the OMB and HUD in helping them to pursue their agenda with other elements of the federal government.

Once we have begun to separate the federal interest in COGs into the stakes that particular federal agencies have, we must become attracted to other points of difference. The OMB is interested in managing the delivery of federal resources. It wants these resources to be delivered in such a way that the federal establishment doesn't look awkward, and it wants these resources, if at all possible, to optimize each other. The great potential of the COG is that it offers some chance for putting the federal government together at the local level in a way that OMB is not able to do at the federal level.

OMB's agenda for the COG is a good and useful one, but not entirely consistent with the interests of HUD and the emerging interests of DOT. HUD is not so much interested in the efficient management of federal resources as it is in the maximization of particular points of view which will enhance regional well-being. For HUD the metropolitan area is the central city writ large. Under the administration of Robert Weaver and George Romney, HUD has had a strong public commitment to racial integration. Planning and action at the metropolitan level (particularly with regard to housing, transit and jobs) is crucial to a racial integrationist strategy. Thus HUD strongly proclaims its interest in regional planning which is comprehensive, which can be implemented, which includes a housing element and which is impacted by citizens (i.e., minority group representatives). These goals may not be objectionable to OMB but they are hardly the same as the tasks implied by the word clearinghouse.

In this early part of the report we do not wish to make too much of the potential differences between HUD and the OMB in the way they view the COG as an instrument of federal policy. We know of no empirical counterparts to the above potential differences. Many HUD staff take great pride in the COG as a communications device and OMB staff are willing to fault the COG on its failures to link planning and the A-95 process. But the other fact is that we know of no COG that has been closed out because of consistent failures to use its plans (if it has any) in the A-95 reviews, and we also know that despite acknowledged failure in utilizing planning as a context for the A-95 process, the process has been broadly expanded. All of which would suggest that both HUD and the OMB are prepared to live with their knowledge that the COG (unless it has been granted authority by the state or unless the clearinghouse rests on the base of a single metropolitan government) is blocked by its structure from systematically using *regional* policies as a basis for negative A-95 "review and comment" upon the applications of member governments for federal monies.

Despite the seeming incompatibility between the COG's policy structure and the demands of regional decision making we think it would be a serious error for HUD and the OMB to change their expectations of the

21

COG as a regional planner/policy maker. There *are* problems which seem to be particularly demanding of regional approaches, the COG is a developing form, and the weight of the state government has yet to be felt.

We would argue that the goal of a regional capacity for planning/decision making is the right one, and should not be surrendered in the face of an apparently inappropriate COG structure. The COG should be forced to live with the strain of federal expectations for regional planning and action. In turn, the federal government should be prepared to assess its expectations of the COG in the face of changing state government action in the region.

There is yet another aspect of federal relationship to the COG which has a particularly useful fit to the Department of Transportation. With regard to highway planning, mass transit and airport planning, there is general recognition that all of these functions have a significant metropolitan aspect, and that they are also integrally related to each other as functions. The "generalists" who sit in the Secretary's office in DOT may be more convinced of these interrelationships than those who sit in the department's line agencies (e.g., FHA, UMTA, FAA). The DOT generalists can be aided by a regional planning mechanism, separate from the localities and special authorities which implement DOT programs. Ideally this mechanism should be able to determine from a regional point of view how regional transportation functions ought to be linked to each other. If the DOT generalists were able to support this kind of regional planning function in an organizational location removed from those who normally implement regional programs (e.g., highway departments, rapid transit districts, airport authorities, etc.), they would have a major counterweight to the tendency of specialists in their department to develop protected relationships with specialists at the local (or regional) level. Thus a strong regional planning mechanism could link metropolitan-type transport actions while also strengthening the capacity of the Secretary of DOT to control elements in his own department.

We are fascinated with the potentials of this symbiotic relationship between a strong regional planning mechanism and the generalists in a federal department. Graphically, these potential relationships might be captured in the following way:

POTENTIAL FEDERAL-LOCAL RELATIONSHIPS

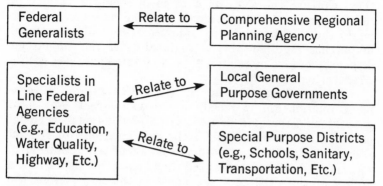

As indicated in the above figure, federal grant relationships tend to flow between federal specialists and local units of action. Federal generalists could use the intelligence manufactured by a regional planning agency to secure control over the specialists within their own department. In effect specialists might be blocked from funding local actions which were inconsistent with the generalist thinking of the regional planning agency, which in turn might be responsive to generalist thinking in the federal agency. This model would also have a particularly good fit to HUD where recent reorganization has attempted to place much greater decision authority in the field into the hands of generalists. It would also be an appropriate model for departments such as HEW and DOT, where the line agencies tend to be ascendant over the generalists in departmental decision making.* The major (and perhaps fatal) problem in the above model is that to this time it has been extremely difficult to develop regional planning agencies which might supply an independent regional point of view in evaluating local applications for federal funds. Both the independence and regional vantage point are characteristically sacrificed when COGs function as protective associations for their local governments in the review process.

In the remainder of this analysis, different patterns of federal involvement with the COG will be recognized. At

---

*The establishment of substate regional planning and development bodies in health, manpower, law enforcement, etc. all engaged in "comprehensive" planning (within a single functional area!) is further evidence of the influence of specialists in federal policy making.

this point it may be useful to conclude that just as the OMB can use the COG as a force in seeing a variety of federal programs from a single regional vantage point, so might the COG be useful to a particular federal department in putting together at the regional level the sometimes disparate actions of relatively powerful line agencies within a federal department.

As we will continuously note, the COG-federal government relationship is hardly a one-way street. For local governments the *quid pro quo* is an obvious one—regional participation in exchange for the continued flow of federal resources. But there are other local agendas in addition to securing federal resources, and they have contributed to the ability of the COG to "take hold" in the majority of the communities we have surveyed. Later sections of the report will attempt to make these other agendas more explicit.

Procedures for Investigation

Four months of intensive field work was carried out amongst three COGs in the western states—the Sacramento area, Puget Sound area and the San Francisco Bay area. Interviews were conducted with staff, key policy people, and the leadership of regional single purpose agencies. COG policy board meetings were attended as well as meetings of standing and *ad hoc* committees.

The three agencies selected for intensive study are all relatively old as COG agencies go. The Puget Sound and Bay Area agencies were among the first COGs established in the country. It was hoped that the maturity of these COGs might expose the study to a different level of problem—those more predictive of what other COGs might soon be experiencing. The possible bias was that these early COGs might reflect a different kind of community receptivity to acting regionally. Sacramento brought the added attraction of being based in the state capitol, and both Seattle and San Francisco are federal headquarter cities.

Because of our interest in interviewing federal personnel we also selected for less intensive study COGs in Chicago and the Dallas-Fort Worth area. Both of these are federal headquarters cities.

Chicago and Sacramento are nominally regional planning commissions rather than COGs. Given the pre-

24

dominance of local government officials in both of these agencies it is difficult to discern any functional difference between these planning commissions and those which are labeled COGs. Perhaps the most noticeable difference is that planning commissions seem to operate under special state legislation which specifies certain expectations with regard to areawide planning.

In addition to Chicago and Dallas-Fort Worth, two other areas were selected for less intensive observation. These were Minneapolis-St. Paul and Jacksonville-Duval County. As a result of state legislation, the Metropolitan Council of Minneapolis-St. Paul is reputed to have more authority to act than any other existing regional council. Jacksonville-Duval is the result of a recent city-county consolidation, where the consolidated government covers the metropolitan area. The agencies observed in Minneapolis-St. Paul and Jacksonville-Duval are the designated OMB clearinghouses for their areas. Interestingly, other well-known recent consolidations in Nashville-Davidson and Indianapolis-Marion are not clearinghouses in that their boundaries do not embrace their metropolitan areas. They were therefore not considered as sites for possible visiting.

In the four less intensively visited areas interviews were always conducted with members of staff, key local government officials, federal officials (in headquarters cities) and staff of regional single purpose agencies. Efforts were also made to see minority group leadership familiar with or active on the COG/clearinghouse in all seven areas. These efforts were not always successful.

Agencies were almost uniformly cooperative and interested in the study. All interviewees were told that statements would not be attributed to them nor would specific agency actions be mentioned in the report, in that this was to be an analysis of issues not a comparison of agencies.

Extensive interviews were conducted with many state officials in Sacramento as well as other state officials based in the areas visited. The executive directors of the Metropolitan Washington COG and the Southern California Association of Governments were also interviewed as were a great variety of federal officials in Washington, and staff members and officials of the National Service to Regional Councils. Parenthetically we should note that almost all of those interviewed warmed to the subject easily. COGs and the problems of regionalism are easy to talk about—perhaps because the governing problems at the regional level are so visible to everyone working in the area. And because of the general recognition that things are going to happen and everyone wants to influence the predicted development of COGs.

NOTES

1 Norton Long, "The Future of the Metropolis," *Crossroad Papers*, Hans Morgenthau (ed.) W. W. Norton, 1965, pp. 112, 121.
2 Richard Cloward and Francis Fox Piven, "Black Control of Cities," *The New Republic*, September 30, 1967, p. 20.
3 See Committee for Economic Development, *Reshaping Government in Metropolitan Areas*, February 1970, for a strong statement in regard to the benefits of two-tiered metropolitan governance.
4 See John Bollens and Henry Schmandt, *The Metropolis*, Harper & Row, 1965, pp. 308-338, for a detailed attempt to distinguish local from areawide activities.
5 H. Paul Friesema, "Interjurisdictional Agreements in Metropolitan Areas," *Administrative Science Quarterly*, June 1970, p. 246.
6 Walter Scheiber, "Evolving a Policy Process for a Metropolitan Region," *Public Administration Review*, September 1967, p. 261.
7 Reynolds Farley, "Changing Distribution of Negroes Within Metropolitan Areas," *American Journal of Sociology*, January 1970, p. 526.
8 Stanley Scott and John Bollens, *Governing a Metropolitan Region: The San Francisco Bay Area*, Institute of Governmental Studies, University of California, Berkeley, 1968, p. 86.
9 *The New York Times*, April 19, 1970.

III. THE ORGANIZATIONAL ENVIRONMENT OF COGS

In an earlier part of this book we noted the confusion of expectations which surrounds COGs. In this section we will provide further detail with regard to these expectations as well as describe the regional actions of various forces in the environment of COG. We have conceived these environmental forces to be: (1) the federal government, (2) the state government, (3) local government, (4) single-purpose agencies, and (5) minority groups.

The Federal Government

No matter what data one uses to describe the federal presence in the metropolitan area the net impact is most impressive (although perhaps less so when viewed in terms of the scope of problems being addressed and the fact that few of these problems can any longer be described as purely local in character). If the clearinghouse is conceived of as a coordinating agency, it needs to compete with the local recipients of four federal agencies which make five different "policy and coordinative planning grants." If one sees the effectiveness of COG's coordination dependent upon its planning capacities then one should know that functional planning grants are made to local grantees through 29 federal programs operated out of 9 different federal agencies.[1] The implementation of these grants creates the local arena within which the COG's capacity to survive and be influential must be tested.

It is by now a commonplace to note the pervasiveness of support for planning in a society where not long ago the very word was connotative of socialism. We have not let the niceties of rhetoric block us from the simple logic that, prior to action, we ought to know what we are trying to achieve, the varied possible routes for achievement, and the rationale for the route we have selected to reach our goals. In addition to discovering the utility of planning (or what passes for planning in many federally funded programs) federal agencies, along with the rest of us, discovered the notion of "comprehensive." In our metropolitan areas everything became connected to everything else (or so it seemed) and therefore federal agencies began to insist that functional planning grants be comprehensive. The thinking and action becomes somewhat tortured at this point but what we emerge with are at least four patterns in federal planning grants: (1) the plain old functional planning grant; (2) the functional planning grant which is supposed to demonstrate its cognizance of everything which might influence the realization of the plan; (3) the policy coordination grant which is supposed to plan for the coordination of a number of actions in the same or related functional areas; and (4) for lack of a better description, the "super" (or synoptic) comprehensive grant which is supposed to provide a framework in which all other planning actions can be seen as rational or irrational. One of these super planning agencies is presumably the COG.

The above is not necessarily an irrational system, but the relative independence of various federal actions from each other (and at times the relative independence of actions within a federal agency) confront the COG with a regional terrain which can seem almost impossible to put in order. These various federal planning grants go to a variety of forces in local and state government, as well as to independent and quasi-governmental agencies. Important client/constituency lines develop between federal agencies and local grantees which impose serious constraints on the COG as, and if, it attempts to become the super comprehensive planner for the metropolitan area.

This report says nothing new in noting the omnipresence of the federal government in support of programs in the metropolitan area. Where federal programs use some criteria of need in making grants (as opposed to grants which are made on a population or first come, first served basis) we would argue that federal actions are the major factor affecting the redistribution of resources in metropolitan areas. In fact any serious effort to undercut the categorical grant system could be seen as negating efforts at redistribution. For example, a program of revenue sharing which eliminated many categorical programs without providing federal standards pushing the expenditure of "shared" revenue in the direction of need would work against redistribution.

In the same way, a federally inspired review process (such as A-95) which was aggressive in making negative evaluations, and whose negative evaluations served to constrain customary federal action, might have the net effect of countering federal efforts at redistribution. At this time a generally bland A-95 review process in effect lets normal federal funding patterns prevail. Those federal programs which tended to be redistributive, remain so.

There is one small clue in another direction. The A-95 process is not uniformly bland. There is a general discontent among COG leadership with competing regional planning agencies, particularly where these agencies are only marginally influenced by local governments (e.g., comprehensive health planning agencies, economic development districts, community action agencies, etc.). Not surprisingly many of these competing regional planning agencies are heavily supported with federal funds and have a primary orientation to change and redistribution. It would indeed be ironic if the most accessible target for COG influence became those federally supported projects concerned with the issues of redistribution.

We have argued that the federal government has been the major factor on the metropolitan scene with regard to issues of redistribution. In performing this role the federal government may have attenuated any major push toward metropolitan reorganization. Federal intervention permits and sustains the areal specialization so typical of the metropolis, by transferring resources from the rich to the poor (communities and individuals), and thus performing some of the painful acts of government which a single metropolitan government might be called on to handle.*

The sum of this argument may be a strange and uncomfortable one to the admirer of the COG/clearinghouse. It is that the A-95 process may need to be watched against the possibility that it would interfere with the tendency of certain federal categorical grants to be redistributive in result.

---

*Even with a single metropolitan government, an important purpose of federal intervention would be to continue to engage in the redistributions which are often too difficult to make by the smallest and most accessible units of government, including a metropolitan level of government.

If federal funds often act to sustain some "balance" in metropolitan areas between rich and poor communities (and between the rich and the poor within communities), federal policy is also (on paper) interested in seeing that federal actions are "rational" from a regional point of view. The Federal Highway Act of 1962 indicates that highway projects will not be approved unless they are based on a continuing comprehensive regional planning process. Federal water quality regulations permit grant requests for waste water treatment facilities to be rewarded only if based on effective regional planning. These requirements seem to be typical of guidelines in most federal programs which deal with regionally oriented resources.

Federal officials, particularly those based in the field, are sophisticated with regard to the issues of regionalism. Where political opportunities and staff time permit, federal staff have generally been able to appreciate the regional implications of federal action. This may account for the slowness and disinterest with which some federal agencies have responded to the A-95 process. Good federal staff have an acute sense of regional issues and may be less politically constrained than COG staff in their expression of these issues.

What federal staff do not yet have is the capacity to order their interventions so that they supplement and complement other federal efforts. And what they *cannot* have is a plan (including an ordered statement of local values) as to how to deal with the developmental issues facing a particular metropolitan area. And this is precisely the area where the best developments in regional governance hold the most promise. At this time the variety of potential federal interventions represent some ordering of national priorities (the federal budget is seen as exemplifying a plan, if you will). In the case of categorical grants some unit of local government (or other appropriate grantee) has to decide that it wants to use federal resources in fulfillment of local goals.

The COG/clearinghouse idea embodies the assumption that national legislation coupled with local willingness to use that legislation does not necessarily constitute a rational pattern of action from the regional point of view. The COG has to attest to that rationality, hopefully within the context of a regional plan. The present reality is somewhat different. Adopted regional plans (which are genuinely regional rather than a collation of local plans) rarely exist, and COGs/clearinghouses most often act to facilitate the flow of federal funds to their local members rather than to influence the use of these funds so that they are instrumental toward achieving regional plans.

The apparent stress in the above analysis on regional planning as an instrument for rationalizing federal action ought not to be oversold. Even if federal practice was to force an A-95 process which relied on adopted regional plans as a basis for review, it is entirely possible that the plans used would be "motherhood" statements—magnificently nonspecific and nonabrasive; able to serve as the cover for approving almost anything. There is some experience in this regard. The requirement for comprehensive regional highway planning has not served to block any federal flow of funds, and almost all water and sewer grants are deemed to be consistent with regional planning so as to be eligible for a 10 percent bonus provision in federal funding. In effect the requirements for regional planning in these two instances were diluted to the point where they do not help in distinguishing "good" and "bad" actions from a regional point of view. Despite these experiences, HUD seems to be moving rapidly toward certifying areawide planning organizations whose planning will serve as the context for future water and sewer and open space grants.

We would not fault this movement by HUD toward areawide planning, just as we remain strongly in favor of the idea of metropolitan development planning. It seems entirely rational to want to expend federal resources (consistent with federal standards) in ways that would maximize metropolitan well-being. Federal policy ought to continue to support the production of intelligence at the regional level which tells us what is meant by "well-being." But can we develop the kind of organizational structure which can produce an intelligence able to order regional action without compromising the general tendency of federal grants to foster metropolitan redistribution?

A recent court of appeals ruling, if eventually reflected in federal legislation or administrative guidelines, would create exciting new potentials for a combined approach to regional planning and federal redistributive efforts.[2] This ruling found a southern municipality guilty of having systematically neglected the physical development of certain of its poor black areas of residence. If federal guidelines were redrafted to favor the upgrading of all such areas as a first order of priority, and if the problem of local matching funds were solved, the regional planning agency might be charged with developing a plan to bring all public amenities in a metropolitan area up to a particular standard.

We think the case is amply made that to talk regionalism is to be attracted immediately to the role of the federal government. We see the federal government as the major metropolitan force for resource distribution. We see the federal government as the principal supporter of regional planning and the prime force involved in sanctioning and financially supporting the COG as a regional mechanism.

We have previously suggested that different elements of the federal government have divergent goals with regard to the utility of a regional mechanism. These goals are not only divergent between agencies but within agencies. With this kind of chaotic federal agency environment it may not be unexpected that the COG would emerge as a bland mechanism. As a new organization, enormously dependent upon its supporters, the COG apparently has chosen a path which would be minimally abrasive to its federal sponsors and to its local members. But this may not be the path to survival. The federal government continues to look clumsy at the local level, and a strong federal OMB must become increasingly impatient with this clumsiness. While the OMB lacks a presence in the field, it has been instrumental in the development of and participation in Federal Regional Councils. These councils appear to be on the verge of discovering the relevance of the A-95 process for their own agenda, and we shall have more to say about this potential relationship.

At this point the federal environment of the COG continues to hold the bulk of its resources, and the key to whatever authority resides in the COG via the A-95 process. But this federal environment is not entirely benign to the COG. To quote one COG director, "the federal government is forcing us into damaging situations of conflict with our own [governmental] membership." It is also clear that further conflict will arise as regional planning matures and if HUD and/or OMB demands that this planning be a condition of the A-95 review process. Later in the paper it will be argued that a COG's willingness to use its own adopted

32

plans should become the price for continued support of the COG by HUD and recognition by OMB.

The State Government

In analyzing the relationship of the federal government to COGs, we made much of a confusion of expectations. The same confusion undoubtedly exists between parts of state government and COGs, but it is much less discernible. There is a small majority of states where an element of the state government appears to have made an in-principle commitment to the COG. In these states there is financial support for the COG (but nowhere approaching federal investment), and ideological support for the COG as the primary vehicle for regionally based planning (e.g., criminal justice, comprehensive health, etc.). We have no doubt that even in those state governments considered to be supportive of the COG there are major bureaucratic elements which would prefer that the state have its own regional presence and/or that the state legislature enable the establishment of regional single purpose agencies charged with performing specific tasks. State interest in, and authority over, regional issues generally manifest themselves through existing state bureaucracies and single purpose agencies, not through the COG. Seen a little more finely this latter situation may be reflective of the executive-legislative split in state government. Single purpose agencies tend to be a legislative response to regional issues whereas the extension of state bureaucratic domain is an executive department response.

If the future role of the state with regard to regionalism is an unknown, it is not an unknown which can be ignored. The question of authority is one which occupies every COG, and the resolution of that question lies at the state level.* Further, the state is the one local government, in place now, whose domain includes the whole metropolitan area (except for areas covering two or more states).

---

*COGs in states with joint powers legislation could conceivably use that legislation as a base for the formation of a regional home-rule agency. Practically speaking the tactic would be impossible in that the agency could only act by unanimous agreement. Or the federal government might partially resolve the authority dilemma by giving to COGs a veto over all federal action on regional type issues. Not impossible—but unlikely.

Some examples of the varieties of state action at the regional level may be indicative of the complexities of the state influenced environment for the COG:

(a) The establishment of regional service districts by the state induces a great variety of state agencies to conform their regional boundaries to these service districts. In some cases state agencies operating in regional service districts will develop local policy making or advisory groups. The more likely case of course is for state agencies to carve out their own unique service areas. (The problems of bureaucratic entrepreneurship seem even more severe at the state level than they are in the federal government. Ironically, in the past it has been federal funds, granted directly to state functional departments, which contributed to this entrepreneurship. Aspects of the A-95 process are meant to arrest this practice, if the governor wants to move in this direction.)

(b) Apart from being state administrative districts, a great number of counties have sought and won home-rule authority for county government, particularly over unincorporated areas. In other cases, where the county fairly well approximates the metropolitan area, the state may become the prime mover of a city-county consolidation such as has occurred in Indianapolis-Marion County, Indiana. The state-designated regional service district in reality is a reinvention of the county as an administrative base.

(c) Various elements in state government, in the process of administering state (or federal) funds, may establish a regional base. Or the federal funds may go directly to the regional agency, provided it has been sanctioned for receipt of these funds by the state agency. In both cases the net result may be an important new regional presence with which the COG has to contend.

(d) States may establish regional special purpose districts or pass enabling legislation which allows their establishment by local action. It is the growth of special purpose districts which has aroused so much concern in local government. We will detail these kinds of agencies as part of the COG's environment in a separate section of this report.

Part of the problem existing between the COG and state government is a lack of commonly accepted definitions as to what a region is as well as what regional issues are. There is a vacuum for governmental action lying somewhere between the city, the county and the state.* One needs to determine empirically whether this vacuum is being filled by aggressive state agencies, by cooperative arrangements between governments, by single purpose multijurisdictional agencies or by the federal government (sometimes in alliance with local government through the vehicle of the COG). In the nature of American government, it would seem that the prerogative for filling the regional vacuum rests with the state government. It is a prerogative which has apparently not been accepted yet. In part the problem may stem from the lack of a common definition as to how or whether a region ought to be governed. Apart from those who favor some form of two-tiered government in a metropolitan area, the literature seems to be influenced by those who discern beneath the seeming governmental chaos an order and stability buttressed by voluntary intergovernmental cooperation which is sufficiently satisfactory to mute the issues of regional governance.

Except in those few states where a comprehensible position toward regionalism seems to be emerging, the COG must deal with the state government as an erratic but always potentially powerful part of its environment. The state can act to bring the boundaries of regional planning and state agencies into conformance with those of the COG, or as in the more likely case of California it can do nothing and foster a situation where there are over 20 different regional boundary patterns for planning and action agencies. The state can enable the creation of single purpose agencies which are subsequently forced to take account of regional positions (as in the Minneapolis-St. Paul area), or it can create state planning operations with

*One can no longer be comfortable with the thesis that the vacuum is well filled through the private and continuing working relationships between local governments. The growth of multijurisdictional single purpose agencies and the growth of federal actions specifying a multijurisdictional base suggest that voluntary intergovernmental arrangements have not worked well enough. But the basic flaw in the voluntary arrangement is that it is voluntary. Many issues requiring regional decisions simply do not lend themselves to the consensual format of a voluntary arrangement.

regional counterparts which may plan parallel to (and at times in opposition to) the COG.

The current difficulties surrounding regional criminal justice planning may exemplify the problems of the COG in relation to the state. In receiving block grant funds under the Safe Streets Act, states were given federal guidelines which seemed to favor regional planning and action. The act authorizes state plans to "encourage units of local government to combine or provide for cooperative arrangements." Based on an 11-state survey, the Urban Coalition pronounced the regional arrangements developed to administer the Safe Streets Act as failures.[3]

Our own observation tends to support this conclusion. In many instances in the 11 states surveyed by the Urban Coalition and in the six states we visited, COGs were grantees of the state for regional criminal justice planning funds. The failures in criminal justice planning may have done great harm to the assumed capacity of the COG to engage in other kinds of regional planning. If these failures dampen the willingness of state governments to use regional planning mechanisms, a major opportunity to develop regional governing capacities will have been lost.

With the current proposals for major special federal revenue sharing to states in six functional areas, there is once again talk of the states turning over the planning tasks to regional agencies. We would suggest that COGs need a better sense of the regional role they wish to play and what roles their structure fits them for before they rush into new situations as arms of a poorly conceived state planning and action system.

In this analysis of the state as a crucial part of the COG's environment we are more taken with the potentials of that relationship than its actuality. Either through a series of *ad hoc* decisions or a major spelling out of the philosophy of state government, it will be up to the state government to determine the character of metropolitan area government. It is our feeling that the aggressive involvement of the federal government has not so much preempted the issue as it has forced the grounds and the timing of state action.

The basic options for state action are: (a) inaction—perpetuation of the current situation of rising federal influence, a growth in single purpose agencies, and erratic regional action by some state agencies; (b) enabling the possibility of regional home rule through multipurpose agencies whose directors are state appointed, directly elected or representative of local government; (c) a rearrangement of county lines, or the establishment of new regional service districts as the basis for state agency action; and (d) the formation of regional umbrella-type agencies having policy control over single purpose agencies, with policy boards directly elected or appointed by the governor, the legislature, or local governments. These four patterns hardly exhaust the situation—but perhaps they make clear that the crucial choice is one of where the primary control of regional decision making shall rest—local government, state government or a new regional political base through a system of direct elections. Whatever decision the state makes, it is likely that by virtue of available resources the federal government will remain a point of great power in regional issues.

Local Government

After four months of observation, in the context of a fair number of years of experience, we are tempted to say that the "moving equilibrium" which sustains fragmented local government is about to move much faster and perhaps the equilibrium is about to become undone. But of course the metropolitan scene has appeared on the verge of becoming governmentally undone for a rather long time. There is a reasonable counteranalysis which suggests that the current metropolitan governing scene will linger on because it offers too many "goodies" for too many people. In the current situation the specialized suburban areas seem to offer some boundary protection to the white middle class; the central city seems within the grasp of black leadership; state legislatures can be kept busy winning friends and doing good deeds by creating programmatically effective single purpose agencies; the state can keep its official distance from troubled metropolitan areas; counties can grow in importance as the most readily available regional type government; and the federal establishment can move between the interstices with its massive resources, performing the redistributive functions which might be expected from a genuine regional government.

37

The only problem with the above "everybody wins" analysis, is that all of the actors on the scene recognize that it doesn't work very well and that its perpetuation is both the symptom and the cause of some of the things which ail us as a society. The result is a deep ambivalence by local officials about the governmental plight of the regions that they live in.* It is difficult to recall a single interview with a local government official where his privately expressed pessimism about the current structure for dealing with metropolitan problems matched his public action in seeking to change an apparently ineffective COG mechanism.

The current scene holds the following additional attractions for local government: big central city mayors know that the road to Washington for them as big cities is often paved with special monies; smaller suburban areas know that they are in the best position to continue to raise their tax base through the relocation and expansion of industry; and many counties are sustained as regional administrative devices although their boundaries are rendered meaningless by the patterns of metropolitan growth.

Given their stakes in the existing order it is not surprising to find local government most comfortable with a conception which sees the COG as an integral part of local government—not a thing apart.** We find this an interesting tactic. When faced with a troublesome and potentially hostile development (regional governance) the local government tactic seems to be to embrace the development so that it is not conceived as an autonomous entity. The evidence for the success of this tactic is rather strong. In the clearinghouses we observed we know of no action taken under the A-95 review process which could be construed as harmful to a local

---

*Raymond Remy, director of the Southern California Association of Governments, focuses the issue more sharply. In response to a draft of this report, he wrote: "If local governments were faced with an either/or choice as to whether they wished to fashion their own organization and be given the tools necessary for meaningful regional involvement or whether they wished to turn over these responsibilities to state or federal levels, then local governments will be placed to the fair test . . . local government officials have not been forced into making difficult regional decisions nor have their political jurisdictions requested them to do so."

**California Assemblyman John Knox verifies this urge by local government to see regional government as an extension of itself. He has written that legislation to establish regional home rule in the San Francisco Bay Area was torpedoed in 1969 because local government would not surrender *any* of the policy control of the proposed regional agency to the process of direct elections.[4]

member government on an important issue. (There are A-95 review processes where the COG staff checks to see that requests for federal funds are consistent with local planning.)

As already indicated, there are several factors straining the COG's current structure. The seeming ability of local government to co-opt the clearinghouse may soon run its course. Local governments are not of a single mind as they look at their region. There are certain natural divergencies in interest between large and small cities, between cities and counties, between regionalists and localists, etc. We think the surfacing of these divergencies could be enhanced by the movement in many COGs to population-weighted, rather than unit-of-government, voting schemes. (Although we have seen no evidence that COGs with population-weighted voting systems have any greater tendency to act without a consensus.) And all of these potential strains toward regionalism can be abetted by a federal policy which insists on an active regional planning/evaluation process as the price for continued federal support of the COG.

We ought not leave this look at local government with the impression of a field of equally competing forces in the metropolitan area that are most advantaged by the status quo. We think the evidence is strong that the federal government, and increasingly the state government, may no longer be prepared to accept a regional balance of government which is unable to govern on regional issues. But there is additional evidence that the big city, the heart and the identity of the metropolitan area (even when outnumbered by its suburban population) is a very special force in the regional environment. In attempting to capture this capacity, Danielson wrote, "Superior capabilities, and the ability to mobilize interests from all parts of the nation, and a sustained interest in broadening the federal government's urban responsibilities, make the central city the most influential participant in federal-metropolitan politics."[5]

The big city is a special force in the COG. Only rarely does the formal leadership of the COG rest with the big city. It is interesting to note the rare number of situations where the big city mayor is a participant in the COG, and instead is represented by a surrogate. But the big city is omnipresent at COG meetings, and while almost always potentially outvoted, the reality never seems to see an issue of consequence in the COG go against the big city. (But this needs to be qualified by again noting that few COG decisions go against anybody.)

To this point the COG seems to have offered no challenge to the big city's regional preeminence. But the potential is clearly there. The City of Cleveland's lawsuit against the COG of which it is a part, alleging discrimination because voting is based on constituent units rather than population, may be indicative of what is to come. The fact that Cleveland's administration was black-led at the time of the suit seemed more than incidental to the situation.

If the predicted black ascendance to political leadership of central cities develops, and if the federal government (or the state) is unwilling to adequately redress the resource position of the residents of central cities, then the "honeymoon" of big and small governments on the COG may come to an end. Black-led central cities could coalesce with other regional "have not" communities, in an attempt to use the A-95 process as a device to force regional redistribution. (However, this is less likely at present when issues of common cause infrequently surmount feelings about race.)

From this vantage point of redistribution (and all that implies for a more equitable society) all of us need to be wary of any regional mechanism which might dilute the political clout of the central city. It is the central city's effectiveness in pulling in resources from its environment (basically the federal government) that offers the most likelihood of redistribution. Any regional mechanism which interfered with federal redistributive efforts so that population criteria or unit of government criteria, as opposed to need criteria, took effect would be severely damaging to the interests of poor people. However if the regional mechanism (on its own or with federal urging) was able to effectively create housing opportunities for poor people throughout a region, the COG could become a force for redistribution. And this occurrence, given the current structure of COGs, seems as unlikely as a COG priority system which would consistently favor the low income populations of central cities.

We come to the conclusion that until the COG (or other regional mechanism) is prepared to be a force in the redistribution of the incidence of urban problems (and of resources to deal with these problems), it is crucial to retain the clout of the central city in its special access to the federal government for monies. The special needs of the central city ought not to be submerged in the name of regional governance.

Single Purpose Agencies

We have already noted Walter Scheiber's observation that "in creating a series of regionwide single purpose authorities we are actually beginning to build the very metropolitan government that many people fear. . . ."[6] But if these single purpose agencies permit the doing of those things which are most appropriately regional without invoking for the electorate the monster of regional government, what is the loss? In the San Francisco Bay area, the Bay Conservation and Development Commission (BCDC) exists as a model of effectiveness in accomplishing the single purpose of protecting the bay against fill. And ironically it does this in the historical context of a failure by the COG to get its member governments to enact local legislation which would protect the bay.[7]

The argument often presented is that the placement of single purpose agencies within a single regional policy framework would permit coherent regional action and would allow political tradeoffs to be made. The dilemma is real. We are certain that the poor black residents of San Francisco's Hunters Point would trade a portion of the bay for industrial development productive of jobs. And we are equally certain that conservationists have had their fill of trading the bay or any other part of the environment in the name of progress. And perhaps with equal cogency we might argue that the tradeoffs in creating the BCDC (to regulate bay fill) were already made at the state level when the agency was created—perhaps the most appropriate place for political bargaining affecting the region to take place.

No matter what the rationale for single purpose agencies, it seems clear that they have contributed to a sense of urgency about how to govern a region. The notion of a regional system is not just an academic concoction. Things are interconnected, and their separation into discrete decision-making units makes the business of government damnably difficult. It is a truth worth repeating that decisions made affecting one unit of a system (the locality in the metropolis) are likely to pose constraints for future decisions to be made within that unit.

When one hears local government officials railing against special districts the official is most apt to be talking about those districts which lie entirely within his jurisdiction. The horrendous figures which are usually displayed to indicate the jungle of governments within a metropolitan area generally are built upon the presence of these kinds of special districts. They include sanitary districts, recreation districts, school districts, transit districts, etc. The reasons for their creation rest in tax tactics, the satisfying of special groups, the distrust of general purpose government, and sometimes the basic unwillingness of general purpose government to govern.

Special districts within a local political jurisdiction which critically affect regional development policies are of course a bane to COGs and the subject of much regional planning. But they are not competitive with the COG in the same way that interjurisdictional special purpose agencies are. In fact a COG might find it organizationally more comfortable to live with 50 small sanitary districts operating within city and county lines as opposed to one powerful metropolitan sanitary district.

In terms of the COG's environment we are more interested in describing special purpose agencies which are interjurisdictional. Harold Wise has captured the important differences between these kinds of regional single purpose agencies. He labels them as being either planning agencies; planning and regulatory agencies; or service organizations.[8] We have already mentioned some of the agencies which plan on an interjurisdictional basis. For example, economic development districts (EDD), multi-county community action planning agencies, comprehensive health planning agencies, regional criminal justice planning groups, airport planning groups, etc. Almost all interjurisdictional planning bodies are heavily supported with federal funds. In some cases these "planning" groups have developed successful working relationships with COGs, and in other cases they are part of the COG (or as in the case of some EDDs, they are the organizational base for the COG). These kinds of agencies seem to offer the greatest organizational threat to the COGs' domain as the regional planner, and we would expect that the A-95 process will be increasingly used in an attempt to bring these planning agencies under COG influence.

The regional planning and regulatory agencies seem to be dominated by their state connection, although one doesn't have to scratch very deep to find federal funds in their budget. Examples are water and air pollution control agencies as well as the aforementioned BCDC. The regulatory agencies tend to operate within state and/or federally established standards, and their planning is meant to enable the achievement of these standards. Their regulatory functions reflect the special problems of regionalism in that they operate in areas where the failure of one jurisdiction to conform to a standard tends to undermine the action of adjoining jurisdictions. The regulatory powers which these single purpose agencies hold are potent pieces of authority —they are the essence of regional governance. We know of no instance where the regional regulatory agency operates in the name of and by virtue of the willing surrender of local powers of government. These agencies tend to be established by the state government, or through the will of the local electorate to realize state enabling legislation. The message is rather clear that local governments seem unable to combine in effective self-regulation, and it is unlikely that COGs will be any more successful in implementing regional self-regulation among member governments.*

The multijurisdictional "service" agencies are a vast and somewhat special aspect of the special purpose agency scene. The services they offer tend to be those we have characterized as facilitative of jurisdictional boundary crossing (e.g., transportation, recreation, etc.) or those where issues of scale force the service to a regional level (utility districts, water supply, etc.). One is more likely to find these service-giving agencies with directly elected policy boards. In the Bay Area these boards were characterized by "low political visibility, ineffectual contests against incumbents, and nearly meaningless elections."[10]

---

*The problems of self-regulation in many fields of endeavor have a rather long history. Dr. Lowell Bellin, New York City Deputy Health Commissioner, in pushing for public rather than AMA supported procedures to audit medical practice noted "even the Pope doesn't confess to himself."[9]

To characterize these agencies as service-giving ought not obscure the fact that they do a great deal of planning in areas which directly impinge on the planning being done by COGs. In fact this comment has a redundant quality about it. If single purpose service agencies operate in areas which are genuinely regional in scope, then it seems a given that they will be involved in planning which will duplicate the COGs. Perhaps the point needs to be made because we tend to see planning and service giving as discrete activities, rather than as sequential parts of a process which may or may not be performed in separate organizational locations.

It is very difficult to discern the dominant direction of change with regard to multijurisdictional special purpose agencies. One can safely predict that their numbers will increase. They appear to be generally effective within their decision areas, and they offer state legislatures a readily acceptable device for appearing sensitive to regional problems. The single purpose agency is also more easily accessible to an interested constituency, and it is these special constituencies which often press state legislators for the creation of special districts.

The continued growth of special districts is also likely to enhance the interest of local governments in a regional mechanism (under their control) as a counterweight. We also expect that federal agencies will seek to retain the protected and special status of their regional special purpose grantees. The failure of HEW to support the inclusion of comprehensive health planning in the COG is a case in point. Similarly OEO, the Department of Commerce and the Department of Transportation support the separate planning capacities of their own special constituencies. We have also suggested previously that the retention of these special planning capacities outside of the COG may be supportive of federal efforts at redistribution.

Even though the resolution of the COG-special district relationship is unclear, the fact of the increasing intensity of that relationship is predictable. We have suggested that COGs will be most likely to use the A-95 process to call into question the activities of these multijurisdictional agencies which are not controlled by local governments. As COGs articulate their regional plans they must find that the special purpose regional district is the agency most likely to be taking action which affects the plan's implementation. Again the observation is almost a redundancy; if these

44

special purpose agencies are regional and if the COG's plans are regional, the predictable discrepancies between the two become naturally abrasive and the grounds for action, particularly where the instrument of A-95 is available.

Central City Minorities

We have conceived of aggrieved minorities as a special and crucial part of the COG's environment. In 1967 Cloward and Piven sounded their warning in a series of *New Republic* articles that federal intervention to aid the establishment of metropolitan government would dilute the central city's powers through regionalism at the very time that blacks were on the verge of taking the political control of central cities.[11] Cloward and Piven were not alone in predicting black political control of central cities, but they were premature in seeing federal intervention through the establishment of clearinghouses as any threat to the position of central cities. As previously indicated, we have observed no instance where the COG acted to disadvantage the central city on an issue of importance.

Conversely, aggrieved minorities do not seem to have discovered the COG in the communities that we observed.* And the COGs have had equal difficulty in discovering aggrieved minorities. The overwhelming "whiteness" of COG staff suggests either insensitive management (abetted by a shortage of black technical talent) or a suicidal urge. The equally overwhelming whiteness of COG policy boards has been somewhat tempered by the inclusion of minority leadership on standing and *ad hoc* COG committees. We will deal with this issue of whiteness of the COG in a later section.

The failure of minority communities to discover the COG is hardly universal. But if minority communities have a very limited sum of political resources, why expend it on the COG? Most COGs have not been overly concerned with areas such as jobs, housing, schools, medical care, etc., which are high on minority community agendas. And mi-

---

*The evidence may be much different in cases where the COG includes a major city headed by a black administration. The Cleveland lawsuit against the COG and the involvement of black leadership in the Metropolitan Washington COG suggests that there are differences.

nority leadership has been slow to admit the equally great stakes of their constituents in regional "hardware" issues. Furthermore, is there any particular point in trying to neutralize or influence COG decision making, if the COG has shown little propensity to punish anybody, but rather seeks to reward everybody? It is true that COGs, using 701 planning funds, have been required to develop a housing element. It is true that every housing element description we have read speaks of "expanding opportunities for housing poor and minority group peoples throughout the metropolitan area." And the Miami Valley Regional Planning Commission (Dayton, Ohio) has achieved the feat of having its board adopt low-cost housing dispersal as regional policy. But as the headline of the Dayton paper reporting the event read: "So now what?" The western office of the National Committee Against Discrimination in Housing (NCDH) suggested an interesting answer to Dayton's question in offering to act as a review agent for all housing programs that came under the A-95 process. Presumably the NCDH was interested in developing a plan for low-cost housing dispersal in cooperation with the COG. But the announced unwillingness of the national administration to use federal housing policy to force integration has once again raised questions about housing integration as a goal. Coupled with this, of course, is the continuing ambivalence among black leadership as to whether regional housing integration (as opposed to good housing in the central city) is a goal worth working for.

There are minority leaders who hold out hope for a regional mechanism and point to an agenda which would be useful. California Assemblyman Willie Brown, Jr. notes: "The priorities of the poor are different from those of the affluent—a regional government that concentrates solely on environmental issues distorts the potential of regionalism.[12] If Assemblyman Brown is implying a social planning agenda (and he is) then the evidence is slim that the COG can deliver on the redistributive aspects of that agenda. We are not prepared to say how a "regional government" (as opposed to the COG) would perform in this regard. If we can posit that minority political leadership must be interested in the redistribution of resources, then our analysis suggests that the special relationship of the central city to the federal government, rather than to the COG, holds the greatest short-term payoff for minority leadership.

46

At the same time we find the issues of regionalism very fluid and capable of great change. Certain new arrangements could maximize the central city residents' capacity to use the resources of the entire region (e.g., transport, clear air, clean water, etc.) while at the same time not diluting the political clout of the central city. In some sense this might resemble the two-tiered government arrangement which the Committee for Economic Development has written about.[13] But there is no imperative for regionalism to develop in this direction. It is more likely to happen if minority leadership finds its way into regional affairs. To this point minority leadership seems an insignificant part of the COG's environment.

NOTES

[1] U.S. Government, Task Force on Planning Assistance, *A Federal Planning Assistance Strategy*, Washington, D.C., October 1969, p. 47.
[2] Jack Rosenthal. "An Effort to Banish the Other Side of the Tracks," *New York Times*, Section IV, February 7, 1971, p. 9.
[3] The National Urban Coalition, *Law and Disorder II*, Washington, D.C., (no date), pp. 3-43.
[4] John T. Knox, "State Initiative for Urban Problems," *Western American Assembly on the State and the Urban Crisis*, Randy Hamilton (ed.), The Institute for Local Self-Government, Berkeley, November 1970, p. 9.
[5] Michael Danielson, *Federal-Metropolitan Politics and the Commuter Crisis*, Columbia University Press, New York City, 1965, p. 186.
[6] Scheiber, *op. cit.*, p. 261.
[7] E. Jack Schoop and John E. Hirten, "The San Francisco Bay Plan: Combining Policy with Police Power," *Journal of the American Institute of Planners*, January 1971, pp. 2-10.
[8] Harold Wise, *Recommendations for Action on Multi-County Governmental Organization*, Washington, D.C., January 1971 (mimeographed).
[9] *Wall Street Journal*, December 16, 1970, p. 1.
[10] Scott and Bollens, *op. cit.*, p. 73.
[11] Cloward and Piven, *op. cit.*, pp. 19-21. Also see *The New Republic*, October 6, 1967, pp. 15-19, for second article in series.
[12] Willie Brown, Jr., "Regional Government: Impact on the Poor," in *Toward a Bay Area Regional Organization*, Nathan & Scott (eds.), Institute for Governmental Studies, University of California at Berkeley, 1969, p. 87.
[13] Committee for Economic Development, *op. cit.*, pp. 4-83.

IV. THE A-95 PROCESS AT THE METROPOLITAN LEVEL

Its Operation

The malpractices and the dilemmas of the A-95 process are certainly well known to OMB personnel, and reasonably well known to many COG staff. The basic dilemma is captured by the COG staff member who said "the reviewed can't do the reviewing." Once that is said the rest may be commentary. But with one caveat: the reviewed can do the reviewing so long as their primary concern is intercommunity clearance and so long as they are not judging the fit of locally proposed actions to regional planning. Which may be precisely why the A-95 review process, despite its current anomalies, has been able to survive and even grow. There is not much of a body of regional planning to do the reviewing against, with the result that local government officials sitting on COG boards don't have to assess a community's proposed action against nonexistent regional planning. As a final touch, some ingenious maker of phrases has coined the ubiquitous review judgment which reads: "This proposal is not inconsistent with regional planning." *Catch 22* is that many COGs have no regional planning to which to be inconsistent.

The nonsense described above cannot go on much longer.* Planning is moving ahead, and one day soon COGs will either have to use their plans as the basis for negative comments, or else revise their plans each time they are confronted with the need to make a negative judgment. Or perhaps adopted plans will reflect the more likely tactic of being so broad gauged as to be meaningless. At the point at which either of the above evasions occurs the dilemmas for HUD and OMB staff will be very interesting. If HUD wishes

---

*None of this is to suggest that clearance procedures, carried out well, are not an adequate raison d'etre for the COG. We will make this point in more detail in other sections of the analysis.

to live compatibly with the COG it may once again have to revise its interest in plans which can be implemented and settle for a regional planning process which has better access to rhetoric than to action. And OMB may have to seek protection in the fact of its not being staffed to deal with these kinds of anomalies in the A-95 process.

There is yet another resolution to the dilemma of the "reviewed doing the reviewing." Despite the relatively clear language in Circular A-95 we have heard staff (some) and policy people (more) question whether the real intent of A-95 is to seek conformance between local action and regional planning. This is no small matter, and this aspect of the review process will continue to be troublesome until the OMB is able to deliver sanctions which make clear that the intent of A-95 is coordination in the context of regional plans, not a kind of coordination where the role of the clearinghouse is that of a disinterested third party.

The above injunction to the OMB to clarify the A-95 process is not made casually. We have no doubt that OMB understands the structural difficulties of the COG, and understands that by seeking more than most COGs can deliver in the way of the A-95 process, it may contribute to the demise of the COG.

We will proceed to inventory the achievements, the failures and the dilemmas of the A-95 process as we found them. And then we will recalculate the wisdom of a federal strategy which publicly appears to demand a dual capacity in the clearinghouse to clear and to evaluate against regional plans, while privately it seems prepared to settle for clearance capacities alone.

1. The Achievements of the A-95 Process.

A. Where the COG has a staff capacity, the A-95 process alerts the COG to proposed local actions using federal funds, and initiates a sophisticated clearance system. The COG is able to let potentially affected actors in a region know about the proposed action, and is able to ensure a process of discussion (and even accommodation) which permits the applicant to maximize his objectives while also enhancing (or at least not doing harm to) other regional actors. Our field work does not indicate that this potential for good is as broadly realized as it could be—but there is nothing in the COG's current structure

49

which would block this realization. The clearing-house function can become a major aspect of the federal system, and can in fact help to resolve much of the abuse and clumsiness of categorical grant programs without impairing their great potentials for resource redistribution. We think a COG which did only clearance, and did it well, would be a major governmental resource.

B. There is another major benefit to the A-95 process which is just beginning to be used and understood. It is that aspect of the process which in effect makes local general purpose government into a local clearinghouse for federal activity in its area. We have observed a number of COGs where a proposed action is not "cleared" until there is formal evidence that it has been approved by the affected local governments. The A-95 process requires the regional clearing-house to notify all affected parties to the proposed action. Because the COG is an instrument of local government, that government is generally conceived to be an affected party. When local government has the staff capacity to use the intelligence produced by the A-95 system, there is the likelihood that A-95 could have the major consequence of enhancing the strength of general-purpose government.[1]

C. Where the clearinghouse process is visible to local elected officials, and to local professional staff, it is the best single device we know to educate local government as to the availability and potential utility of federal resources. (From this vantage point there is every reason to put *all* federal *and* state categorical programs under clearinghouse review.)

D. The clearinghouse procedure also creates an interesting possibility for resolving the federal dilemma of how to render effective technical assistance to localities. Federal staff have always been hampered in rendering such assistance because in the process of a locality's asking for federal assistance it is likely to expose its weaknesses, and therefore hurt the locality's competitive position for federal funds. But the COG, *as it now functions*, unlike the federal government, stands in a benign relationship to local government. Experience has shown that the COG almost never acts to hurt local government. But the COG

50

is more than just a friend of local government—it is its instrument; it is conceptually an integral part of local government. Yet it has more breadth of vision about regional problems than does local government. The COG is currently in an ideal position to render technical assistance to localities. And in fact it has begun to do so. We have observed some COGs entering into "Lakewood Plan" type arrangements—that is, where they sell planning and other technical services to small localities. We would recommend that federal agencies conceive of the COG as a technical assistance resource and fund it accordingly. Even if the COGs were to develop a greater willingness to make judgments about grant applications, this need not conflict with a technical assistance role. Presumably the COG's judgments would be about the regional implications of the action, not about the potential effectiveness of the grant application. The latter would remain a federal judgment.*

We think the above four actual and potential achievements of the COG are all the justification that it needs as an institutional resource worthy of support. The problem is that the task of regional governance runs beyond the COG's areas of achievements, and it is some of these tasks (both specified and implied in the A-95 circular) which lead to the dilemmas and failures of the COG.

2. Dilemmas

A. A continuing dilemma is when and if to bring policy people (as opposed to staff) into the A-95 review process. One of the COGs we observed operated on the plausible assumption that it was a staff job to determine when an application conflicted with regional plans. Unfortunately for the logic of this process, this agency had almost no adopted regional plans. As a result staff made policy reviews in a vacuum, and policy people were almost never involved in the review process. Conversely, most agencies we observed aggressively sought to expose their policy people to the review process. But few had solved the administrative dilemma in terms of which applications were "worth" exposing to policy boards.

---

*Despite these distinctions it does seem likely that a COG which began to make negative judgments about local governments would become less able to perform the technical assistance function.

As a result the review process becomes overloaded; everything is worthy of review with the result that nothing is really reviewed with any great depth by policy boards.

B. Another persistent dilemma in the review process is just how far to open up access by nongovernmental groups to applications under review. We have previously noted an interest by the western office of the National Committee Against Discrimination in Housing in reviewing housing items. It is likely that the Sierra Club would want to systematically be involved in commenting upon regional growth projects. We have discerned no particular pattern to who gets involved in the clearance process. The process is in the hands of staff with little policy consideration of the important issues involved. Our strong impression is that staff have taken a constricted view of who to involve in the review process beyond local government. After all, the more the system is opened, the more likely it is to produce negative comment; a result which may not be desired by any of the current parties to the A-95 process.

C. While some of the dilemmas in item B above result from strategic considerations, others that are equally important flow from the meagerness of staff resources which COGs are able to devote to the review process. In a sense, the budgetary support of staff involved with the A-95 process is a "backdoor" item for HUD 701 funding. The more tangible the staff items become in the budget, the more they are open to question. All with the net result of a very undermanned A-95 system. But again this may be considered functional, in that a highly productive staff process might deliver the kind of results (negative recommendations) with which the clearinghouse and the federal government would be unprepared to cope.

D. An additional dilemma has been thrust upon COGs by HUD in its insistence on citizen involvement. Certain COG leadership recognizes the benefits of bringing citizens into the A-95 process; particularly citizens who are representatives of minority interests. But any politician, by definition, knows of the costs involved in bringing new (and perhaps uncontrollable) parties into the decision process. The net result to this point is an apparent immobility in bringing voices to bear upon the clearinghouse process other than elected officials and employees of local government.*

3. Failures

A. The most overwhelming and blatant failure of the A-95 process is its great difficulty in distinguishing between good and bad applications from a regional point of view. On a *de facto* basis everything is good—because the system finds that almost nothing is bad. A major theme of this report is that this inability to make distinctions between applications is a product of the COG's structure—we do not anticipate great changes over time, unless the structure of the COG changes, except with regard to the willingness of the COG to take on other regional planning agencies which are a perceived threat to the COG's domain or which tend to be less influenced by local government in their policy making.

B. The general failure to make distinctions between applications is not meant to indicate that COGs (particularly their staff) are always happy with the current functioning of the A-95 process. There is also a failure by some federal agencies to show any great interest in the process, or to take serious account of the questions which some COGs raise about an application. But we are told by OMB staff that very little of this COG unhappiness with federal agency response is raised to a formal level of protest. The few protest situations we are familiar with concern funds for special purpose districts or for "competitive" regional planning agencies.

C. This widespread federal lack of knowledge and disinterest in the A-95 process also manifests itself in a failure by federal agencies to let COGs know whether they have taken any recognizance of COG comments on an application, or to simply feed back information to the COG as to whether a grant has been made. We think

---

*Because of federal and state guidelines citizen involvement is much more a fact of life in criminal justice and comprehensive health planning activities when these are a part of the COG's in-house activities.

there is the will by federal agencies to do better in the area of information feedback; nevertheless one must wonder why in a technologically competent society it becomes so difficult to complete information loops. Perhaps the will is really not there—or there is a large and continuing failure in federal management.

D. There also seems to be a failure by OMB and by states to clearly establish the COG's prerogatives in reviewing state applications for federal funds. If block grants to states continue and increase in importance, it would be very useful to give a regional mechanism some kind of review leverage over these grants.

E. Other failures of the review process are of smaller proportions; they generally reflect the marginal position of the COG vis-a-vis its governmental members, or the inadequate staff resources devoted to the A-95 process. These failures include: (1) the inability of COGs to insist on their review prerogatives when a major governmental member wants to rush an application through; (2) a tendency to review an application because of its potential effectiveness rather than for its implications for regional coordination and the realization of regional goals; (3) a tendency for reviews to be idiosyncratic rather than based upon established policy—of course the fact that there is little adopted policy in COGs forces the reviews to be idiosyncratic; (4) an apparent lack of site visiting by COG staff to applicant communities. Given the continuing comment that the final A-95 action by the COG is the "tip of the iceberg," we were not impressed with the extent of the activity we were able to see beneath the iceberg. However, there were significant differences between COGs in this respect, and with a decent budget and clarification of function we would anticipate great changes with regard to the clearinghouse aspects of the A-95 process.

F. We also noted the failure of COGs to distinguish the most appropriate times in the review process for the involvement of staff as opposed to policy makers. We have referred to the procedures of one COG which determined that everything was initially staff prerogative, subject to appeal to policy people. The flaw in this agency was that staff had little policy context to operate within. It seems clear that the material that a COG sees in the preapplication "early warning" stage is very different from that which appears in a final application. Both of these application stages would seem to call for different levels of policy and staff review, in accordance with the COG's view of its own role and strength. At present these distinctions are not well made. The timing of staff as opposed to policy involvement seems happenstance; generally a matter of convenience rather than of conception.*

In sum, the achievements of the A-95 process are real and important. They would appear to offer ready validation for the survival and growth of the clearinghouse concept. But the failures of the A-95 process are equally real and important. In our analysis they result from inadequate resources devoted to the review process, and the establishment in Circular A-95 of goals for the review process which are inappropriate to the current structure of the COG. Our recommendations in the face of this analysis are filled with risk for the COG. We favor an explicit commitment by the OMB to two primary roles for the COG: clearinghouse *and* regional planner/evaluator. The clearinghouse role needs most of all a clear and continuing flow of resources to accomplish the job. The planning/evaluation function can only be pursued in very limited situations given the current structure of the COG. The COG's difficulties in this regard surround it with an aura of failure, and that failure may imperil the COG's clearinghouse function as well.

We remain convinced of the need for an agency which can plan regionally and which possesses the authority to implement those plans. The COG is not now that kind of agency. And it is experiencing strain because of some federal expectations to move in that direction. We are not prepared to resolve the dilemma for the COG by recommending the elimination of the planning/evaluation function. The strain the COG is experiencing is good and useful because the COG, with all of its problems, seems to have the best *developmental* potential with regard to be-

---

*William Brussat of the OMB indicates that the preapplication part of the process is really a "screening" rather than a review. It is a very useful distinction, although not one which regularly informs action by the COG.

coming a force for metropolitan governance. We would be prepared to risk losing the clearinghouse capacity if that were the result of continuing federal pressure to use regional planning/evaluation in the A-95 process.* We will deal elsewhere with the implications of these comments.

Planning as the Context for the A-95 Review Process

In the previous section we called for additional action by the OMB to indicate that the review and comment procedure is meant to include an evaluation of applications for federal funds in the light of regional planning. OMB can rightfully point to the existing A-95 document which calls for "information concerning the extent to which the project is consistent with comprehensive planning developed or in the process of development for the metropolitan area." Surely this is a clear enough statement of intent. But the problem is that HUD and OMB have generally failed to manage the resources (money, recognition, technical assistance, etc.) they give to the COG so as to support this stipulation. But we think the problem goes beyond that—we perceive it as a failure to really transmit that the A-95 process is a two-headed one—clearance and evaluation against an adopted regional plan. The COGs which are building their regional plans as a collation of local planning and the COGs which conceive of themselves almost solely as service organizations do not at present appear to be in danger of receiving negative sanctions from HUD or OMB.

None of this is to say that many COGs don't theoretically recognize the important links between the A-95 process and their planning. One COG, in describing its "comprehensive general plan" writes, "if it were not for the requirement that local plans anticipating the use of federal funds must be correlated with the regional plan, it would be hard to point to any meaningful intervention of this plan in the region's problem-making [sic] trends in urban development." Another COG writes, "Since 1966, the [COG] has used the grant review process to implement its regional planning goals and policies." The empirical question is whether these COGs have really been able to use the

---

*We would run the risk to spur the evolution of the COG. If this risk led to the collapse of an individual COG, we feel certain that the clearance procedure would be revived in another form because it is so patently rational and useful.

A-95 process to help in implementing their plans. Our findings seem to say no.

The basic regional planning issue, the one which appears to occupy all general planning being done in COGs, is the one of land use. The land use plan ought to establish a base for "special element" planning which needs to be done for regional type amenities such as transport, sanitation, water, housing, etc. The basic land use issue in the metropolitan area appears to be a continuation of current patterns of scatteration versus some control of growth according to a regionally approved design. Any scheme of land use control, as opposed to the current laissez faire policy of regional scatteration, *if adopted and if implemented,* is likely to be redistributive in effect. It would deal with population densities, land uses for industry, open space, transportation networks, etc. All of which could have a profound effect on each community in a metropolitan area.

If one can predict from current events, it seems likely that COGs using HUD funds will complete the preparation of regional land use plans. In many cases this general plan will simply incorporate local land use plans coupled with some attempt to equitably distribute regional amenities such as parks, open space, transportation, etc. In these cases, where the regional plan embodies local planning, the A-95 process can be used to bring single purpose agency action into conformity with planning by local government. The ironic effect of the A-95 process could be that, in the name of regionalism, it would become a device whereby the COG could undercut those agencies performing regional type functions. As a hypothetical example in the San Francisco Bay area, in the name of supporting a regional land use plan the COG could seek to restrict the capacity of the BCDC to stop the filling of the bay.*

Equally interesting is the situation of the COG which does develop regional plans, but whose plans have limited influence over its member governments. The director of a large regional single purpose agency who felt his agency was being harassed by the COG noted that his agency's requests for funds were reviewed *as if* the COG had the

---

*This is a very hypothetical example in that BCDC is not dependent upon the federal government for funds or authority, and the Bay Area COG's land use plan seems more than a pastiche of local planning.

capacity to implement its general land use plans. He noted that the COG did not have this capacity; development would continue on a scatteration basis and the result would be that his agency (a major sanitary district) could be made by the COG to look as if it were unable to plan effectively for the servicing of regional development as it was *in fact* taking place. T. Jack Kent, who wrote that "a good plan is self-fulfilling,"[2] to the contrary, good regional plans may be perceived as very bad by localities in the region and not fulfilled at all. And as with the above described sanitary district situation the net effect of the good plan could be to block the action of the single purpose regional agency while other local governmental actions circumvented the regional plan.

We admit that much of the material in this section on planning and the A-95 process is speculative. There simply are not enough COGs with a long enough history of adopted plans to make judgments about. But what evidence there is offers no reason to be sanguine. The slowness of COGs in adopting plans is one discouraging fact. The generality of regional planning and its capacity to allow for many different kinds of specific actions are further evidence of the problems in using current products of regional planning as a context for A-95 reviews. The generalized plan can be a point of departure for review—a not insignificant use. But more often one hears the comment, in regions with adopted plans, that "no one ever expects them to be used." In effect the multicolored documents produced may be part of a ritual one goes through to get federal funds—the plans are seen as the property of the COG's staff (or of the federal agencies which paid for them), not of the member governments of the COG.

As in the previous section we are recommending continued support of planning *within* the COGs, despite the accumulated evidence of failure to this point. Our recommendation derives from the imperatives of our previous argument, and the failures in planning we have described above support our argument. Clearance procedures and planning/evaluation are complementary parts of a process. If the COGs are unable to perform the planning/evaluation function on projects affecting their member governments, that inability will become more evident as the planning of the COGs matures.

As the strain on the COGs increases because of their

inability to reconcile their plans with the projects being reviewed under the A-95 process, the likelihood increases that the COGs may evolve into a structure more compatible with the decision making needs of the region. The key assumption in this projection of events leading to breakdown and transformation is that the adopted regional plan must be powerful enough (distinguishing between parts of the region) to be influential. Here, of course, it becomes the continuing task of HUD to certify the fit between proposed regional planning solutions and regional problems. Where this fit does not exist, HUD ought to decertify the COG as an areawide planning organization and OMB ought to dedesignate the agency as a clearinghouse.

Priority Setting

One COG director noted that "we are being pushed to deal with priorities which we are constitutionally unable to accomplish." This parallels the observation that "those being reviewed can't do the reviewing." Any situation which forces a body of peers to make potentially costly distinctions between its own members becomes "constitutionally" difficult. We have previously indicated that this is the essential structural problem of the COGs.

Not surprisingly there is not yet much experience in the COGs with regard to priority setting. Most COG directors recognize it as an "unnatural" act given their structure, and are not rushing to embrace priority setting. But some HUD staff and HUD guidelines see the situation differently. "The evaluation of agency effectiveness should include an analysis of how planning has resulted in an allocation of resources on the basis of socially responsive priorities, has led to a better environment for all persons, or has saved dollars."[3] In this quotation from HUD guidelines, priority setting is seen as an intrinsic part of the planning process. The HUD staff who wrote these guidelines are under the impression that priority setting is precisely what HUD is paying for with 701 planning funds; the ordering of those program actions most important to the attainment of specific regional goals.

Some federal agencies with very limited funds, as measured by the volume of applications for a region, have begun to seek a sense of regional priorities as determined by the COGs. In response to this we have heard COG policy makers express a fear of priority setting which would deprive their region of money because it might go to regions with greater needs. We discount the remark; priority setting is always difficult for the COGs, even where the federal agency guarantees that the available funds will not be transferred to another area.

Apart from an interest by HUD staff in priority setting as part of planning, we have sensed an interest by staff of the Department of Transportation in a local ordering of priorities which would assign some weight to competing transportation modes. A number of other federal agencies have language with regard to priorities in their guidlines, but it is likely that this language is intended to give federal staff a handle for decision making, not to turn priority setting over to local bodies such as the COG.

We are of course back to the fundamental question of regional redistribution. Who would benefit if the COGs rather than the federal agency were to make the basic determinations with regard to priorities? It has been our continuing argument that the COGs would make priorities to insure a rough equity (based on population) between member governments. Conversely, we have argued that the federal agency is better able to make its priorities responsive to need, such as giving special priorities to central cities where needs are often greatest.

We would again note that the issue of attempting to influence priorities as part of the A-95 process is a highly academic one. The regional planning documents we have read deal very superficially with the notion of priorities, and there is no overwhelming display of interest by federal agencies in having the COGs determine priorities. This federal disinterest would be reinforced by reading the comments of one COG in response to the federal agency which asked them to help determine priorities. The COG rejected a priority-setting role, approved all applications under review and wrote to the federal agency, asking that each grant request "be considered *separately* on the individual merits of each application [our emphasis]."

Because of the "constitutional" problems, we think the issue of priorities will continue to bedevil the COGs for as long as they are alive. Priorities are part of planning; if a COG is able to posit regional goals then surely it must have some idea as to which actions best enable the attainment of those goals. We would recommend that federal agencies, and HUD in particular, force the issue of priority setting as an intrinsic part of regional planning. As with the stress induced by planning/evaluation, we think that a focus on priority setting will speed the evolution of the COGs toward a regional governing force.

In urging this focus on priority setting we are mindful that we have already stressed "that until the COG is prepared to be a force in redistribution . . . it is crucial to retain the clout of the central city in its special access to the federal government for money." We do not think that the COG as it is currently structured can be such a force. A federal insistence on priority setting is one of the factors which can help the COGs evolve into a more appropriate structure for regional governance. But even if this evolution takes place, we would place our greatest reliance on the federal government as a force for redistribution. Regional priority setting, even if constitutionally possible, should be carried out in the context of federal standards which assure that federal resources are expended on the communities and individuals with the greatest needs.

Relationships to Local Governments and Other Agencies

We made the point earlier that a COG can be conceived of as an agent of the OMB. When it functions well in its clearinghouse capacities, it helps to perform a federal management task. The task would be aided by the delivery of some supportive action by units of the federal government. In those few cases where COGs are critical of grant applications, federal agencies must let the COG know whether federal action sustained the COGs' criticism. And if the federal agency chose to ignore the COG, the COG must know why.

The gross failures in communication from federal agencies to COGs may reflect the low esteem in which many federal agency staff hold COGs. But this is hardly a uniform situation. COGs know that they are differently valued by different federal agencies and by different organizational units within those agencies. COGs almost invariably see HUD as a friend and DOT as a potential friend. COGs have also learned that the Department of

61

Defense is as impregnable in its domestic relations as it hopes to be abroad. One publicly available piece of correspondence from a DOD official to a COG noted: "I have been instructed to inform you that the Intergovernmental Cooperation Act has not been implemented by the Department of the Army."

COGs need to learn better that there are elements within large federal agencies which have a generalist approach to the management of a department's resources. The COGs need to make alliances with these departmental forces against those elements which see their own function above all. OMB might help by requiring each federal regional office to establish a liaison staff member to help protect the A-95 process in his own department. Departments such as HEW already have a person in the regional director's office assigned to worry about A-95 as part of his concern for intergovernmental relations. The problem for HEW, as in a number of other departments, is that program decision making is centralized in Washington, and even in the region the regional director has inadequate influence over grant recommendations made by functionally oriented offices. The implications for strengthening regional generalists and for moving program decision making to the field are obvious. The OMB might also introduce some checks on the willingness of departments to ignore A-95 comments, by requiring that COGs send copies of all negative A-95 comments to the Federal Regional Council and to the appointed A-95 liaison in the department. Federal agencies in turn should be required to respond to the COGs on all negative reviews. (It is not impossible that the net effect of this kind of more "powerful" A-95 system would be to further depress the capacity to make negative reviews.)

While the federal government is the most significant element in the COGs' current environment, it is with local governments (and independent agencies) that the COGs are the most active. No matter what the level of the COGs' activities, we have found COG action to be a powerful force in creating a sense of community about governmental operations in a metropolitan area. Despite the fact that the possibilities of the system of interjurisdictional clearances have hardly been realized, there is a widespread sense of achievement about the COGs' contribution to a more visible metropolitan community. We are also most impressed with the potential the A-95 process offers for the strengthening of local government influence over actions in the COGs' jurisdiction, but here too the emphasis is on the word potential.

Lastly, any appraisal of the A-95 process as an intergovernmental mechanism must return to the curious role of the state. Despite the federal government's importance to the COGs, it is the state that is the gatekeeper of the COGs' future as a force for regional governance. We have not looked carefully at the operation of the A-95 process at the state level. Such an investigation has been conducted simultaneously with this study by the Council of State Governments. But our general impression is that few, if any, state governments are so structured as to be able to use the A-95 process as a device for implementing state planning (if anything like that exists). If state planning flourished, and if COGs were effective regional planning mechanisms, the need for relationship between the COGs and the state would become even more critical. Obviously those criteria which make an issue regional might just as easily make it of statewide (or interregional) concern.

If the realization of a state-regional planning relationship is somewhat in the future, the relationship with regard to clearance procedures is immediate. Both the state and the region are structurally able to handle the clearance procedure. At the state level, it is, of course, a potentially more powerful procedure because it is connected to an authority source—the governor's office. For clearance procedures to be more effective at both levels there must be more clarity with regard to how intervention takes place when both the state and the region perceive a coordination problem. And routines involving joint action must be worked out which will minimize time delays when an application is of interest to both the state and regional clearinghouse.

We have not paid much attention to the issue of time lags which the A-95 procedure raises in intergovernmental relations. There are needless abrasions, occasioned by sloppy management which discredit the process with large local governments and with federal agencies. We think the OMB can protect the early warning part of the A-95 process while at the same time forcing more rapid movement of reviews. The fact that revised A-95 procedures significantly shorten review time available for certain mortgage loan programs ought to act as a general stimulus for more rapid action.

The key to improved time procedures would seem to be very early decisions on which applications have coordination and policy implications and which don't, and rapid approval of the latter.*

The A-95 Process as a Vehicle for Redistribution

Douglas Harman has written that COGs "must eventually leave the relatively safe environment of comprehensive land use planning and fight the battles over the urban social environment."[4] The imperatives of regional problem analysis may lead Professor Harman to that prediction; however, there is very little in the current structure or the experience of the COGs which would accommodate the redistributive decisions which the social environment demands. In fact there is nothing in our observations which would support Harman's notion that comprehensive land use planning is a "relatively safe environment" for the COGs. It is safe only in-so-far as the COGs we have observed have shown little capacity to use the A-95 process as a vehicle for implementing their land use plans.

We have maintained an apparently contradictory position throughout this report with regard to the issues of redistribution. Our observation has detected very little in the COG experience which would evidence its ability to influence redistribution.** We have concluded that the COG, based as it is on local government membership, is not structurally able to deal with problems of redistribution. Also, we noted that the best possibilities for redistribution lay in federal cash transfers to individuals, in federal taxing policies and in the special funding relationship which large central cities have recently enjoyed with the federal government. We even suggested that a COG which sought to interfere with the central city-federal government relation-

---

*As with other ideas in this section, OMB staff have urged this recommendation upon COGs. The failure to implement recommendations undoubtedly reflect staff resource problems in COGs and the OMB, as well as problems in the structure of the COGs. Careful analysis suggests that staff problems (local and federal) best account for difficulties with clearance procedures, while organizational problems of the COGs better account for their failure as planner/evaluators. The former problems are, of course, more easily remedied.

**Our observations on the Metropolitan Council in Minneapolis-St. Paul and of the Jacksonville-Duval Area Planning Board are of a different order and will be summarized elsewhere in the book.

ship might be acting to negate efforts at redistribution. Then in apparent contradiction to the logic of the above argument, we have recommended that both OMB and HUD retain the expectation that COGs will not only act as clearing agents but that they will evaluate applications for federal funds in the context of their regional planning. It is the federal expectation of regional planning/evaluation as linked to the A-95 process that we predict will place severe strain on the COGs and speed their evolution to a more powerful regional governing form or contribute to the COG's demise.

The contradictions in the above analysis are that it appears to force greater activity on issues of redistribution by a mechanism (the COG) whose structure inclines it to distribute resources "equitably" to all of its members. *These contradictions in our recommendations are meant to achieve two purposes: to emphasize the primary role of the federal government as a force for redistribution and to strain the COG to deal with an issue which it is structurally ill-equipped to pursue.*

Currently, the COGs appear to handle the strain inherent in the above situation by rarely acting on the negative implications of their planning/evaluation tasks. The COGs apparently choose not to interfere with the flow of federal resources to local governments. In that way the redistributive tendencies of federal programs are protected and so are the COGs. The results are benign for everyone provided that one discounts the need for an overall regional decision making force which can make distinctions between local governments. At this point it is most likely the single-purpose regional agency, empowered by the state, which has the capacity to govern regionally. While there is a certain equilibrium in the current situation, in part owing to the real capacity of many single purpose agencies, the situation of regional governance is inherently unstable. Local governments become increasingly unhappy in the face of powerful regional single purpose agencies while state governments continue to use the single purpose agency option to deal with regional problems. On top of this the federal government has to decide whether it is simply interested in a regional clearance mechanism, or one which is forced into acts of governance. The regional scene is indeed alive with change and new expectations. Only as the federal (and possibly the state) government helps the COG/

clearinghouse to remain at the center of these changes and expectations can the COG be a force in the evolution of the kind of governing capacity that our metropolitan problems require.

NOTES

[1] William Morgan, "Memorandum to Richard Langendorf," Director of Planning and Evaluation, Model Cities Administration, Department of Housing and Urban Development, January 27, 1971 (mimeographed).
[2] T. Jack Kent, *The Urban General Plan*, Chandler, 1964, p. 78.
[3] Department of Housing and Urban Development, "Memorandum on Funding Program for Comprehensive Planning Assistance—Fiscal Year 1970," October 7, 1969, p. 11.
[4] B. Douglas Harman, "Councils of Governments and Metropolitan Decision Making," *1969 Municipal Yearbook.* p. 16.

V. THE CHARACTER OF REGIONAL DECISION MAKING

In formulating our observations for this section of the report we are struck by a pervasive question. Why do key local public officials and high level staff contribute so much of their time to an organization without authority? The character of public decision making in the COG is no match to the caliber of men and women engaged in the process. Then why do they engage in it? One obvious reason is that there is a community of interest—the metropolitan area is not just a Census Bureau notion—there are interdependencies which demand communication if nothing else. Secondly, the COG is a potentially useful arena to those political figures with larger aspirations—there are issues on which one can look like a regional "statesman" without necessarily damaging vote-getting capacity at home. There is also a fairly well-established norm that governments ought to appear to be cooperative—and participation in the COG is a useful way to demonstrate cooperativeness. Lastly, and perhaps most importantly, local governments participate because of the common assumption that their federal grant-getting capacities would be damaged if they absented themselves.

Local governments participate in the COG because they expect to benefit; they want to communicate with their neighbors, to appear cooperative, to be (or remain) eligible for federal funds and at times to create the appearance of an effective regional mechanism so as to stall state action in the region. Local governments have no expectations that participation in the COG will be harmful to them. Thus the decision making norm that emerges is action by consensus— all parties must publicly agree that the COG's decisions will not be costly to them. Perhaps a recounting of comments by COG staff members about COG decision making patterns will better make the point. "We exhibit a log rolling style of decision making"; "we are a service agency, not a big stick"; "we are in no position to be tough on anything";

67

"the COG is set up to be protective, not to have influence." Erie, Kirlin and Rabinovitz in their survey of regional mechanisms capture this bland quality of the COG best by noting that "a decision making norm results which is designed to maintain the continued operation of the area-wide institution by not threatening the subunits."[1]

The governmental representative who sits on the COG is a delegate of a subunit. He is not there to move an issue, but rather to protect and hopefully enhance the interests of the area that he represents. None of this is to argue that there are not differences among delegates to the COG. If we were developing types, surely some would resemble regionalists as opposed to others who are more locally oriented.* In some cases, being named to sit on the COG is considered more of a chore than an honor, and those who agree to serve tend to be the most regionally oriented members of their local government bodies. We have even seen an attitude survey which indicated that a large number of COG policy people, if faced with an issue which would enhance the region while hurting their locality, said they would take the regional point of view. Nothing in our experience validates this attitudinal data—yet the value it displays is an interesting one, reflective of norms favoring regional cooperation.

The COG is not totally bland. We have noted situations where the recommendation of the COG, if sustained by the federal granting agency, would be hurtful to certain local parties. But in our observation, almost invariably these "local parties" turn out to be regional planning agencies, which can be viewed as competitive with the COG, or single purpose agencies whose actions are not favored by local general purpose governments.

If one were to draw a model of decision making which was most compatible with the structure of the COG, it would need to be one where members of the COG all stand to benefit (i.e., service-giving decisions) or where a decision is helpful to some while not necessarily hurting others. Thus COG decisions which might block members from getting desired resources are "unnatural." In the same way COG decisions/recommendations which would contribute to a regional redistribution of problems or the redistribu-

---

*We use the notion of "regionalist" as denoting a position favoring a regional decision making capacity.

tion of resources could be seen as equally unnatural to the COG as currently structured. But with one important caveat: we thing that effective COG leadership (backed by explicit federal expectations) could develop a *quid pro quo* as a result of which the COG would not attempt to redistribute problems and in exchange would focus on redistribution of resources. In effect the COG could function to sustain the areal specialization (see definition below) of a metropolitan area by planning for and sanctioning "inequitable" flows of federal money to deal with problems *where they are.* For example, the COG might develop a priority system favoring water and sewer grants for the most deprived areas of a region, while local bonding capacities were used to bring pipelines to new suburban areas of growth. Or the COG could shape its regional transportation planning network to give central city residents subsidized and efficient transportation to suburban jobs as a functional substitute for placing low-cost public housing in suburbs.[2]

Needless to say the above analysis brings us directly into the issues of black, brown and white. Oliver Williams & Associates in their book, *Suburban Differences and Metropolitan Policies*, characterize the "metropolitan problem [as] the unequal distribution of resources and services that result from the process of [areal] specialization."[3] Williams & Associates use the term "areal specialization" as a euphemism for a pattern of governmental incorporation in metropolitan areas which tends to reflect class and racial differences. Their approach to this pattern is not to break it (i.e., areal specialization) but rather to equalize the distribution of resources and services to these specialized areas. The net short-term result would be to leave the blacks and browns where they are—in the central city and in ghettoized suburban pockets—but with more equal access to jobs, to good schools, to good housing. It is a mean tradeoff, but one which can be made, and one which the COG as a mechanism can be instrumental in helping to make.

The conditions for the tradeoff are: (1) effective COG leadership which can articulate the terms of the tradeoff— a redistribution of resources in return for sustaining an areal specialization of problems; and (2) a large flow of federal dollars to metropolitan areas so that the redistribution is based upon new resources from the outside—not the redistribution of existing resources inside the metropolitan area; and (3) the presence of strong minority leadership in the COG who can opt for the terms of the tradeoff as a public policy choice.[4]

It is likely that we shall find a public opting for areal specialization coupled with the redistribution of public resources too difficult. It is an option at great variance with our professed norms of an integrated society. But we wonder if the current situation of *immobilisme* on racial matters is the tactic best calculated to help us make it as a society. We think that regional governing mechanisms (including the COG) are particularly suited to surfacing the decision issues surrounding a tradeoff between the distribution of problems and resources. We think regional plans, if they are forced to meet some criteria of potential impact on regional problems, must opt for resource or problem redistribution (or a combination of both). And it is for this reason that we will urge throughout this report that the OMB and HUD sustain a pressure on the COG to make regional plans and use them as the basis for the A-95 review process.

In a number of places in this report we have alluded to a different character of decision making in the Metropolitan Council of the Twin Cities area and in the Jacksonville-Duval Area Planning Board. The Metropolitan Council is the only clearinghouse we have observed which is not a COG.* It is also the only clearinghouse we have observed which is involved with the issue of fiscal disparities in the metropolitan area. The Metropolitan Council has prepared legislation for state action in this regard. The Metropolitan Council is also working on an extremely important plan to use the construction of a major new airport as the basis for regional tax redistribution. A current proposal is for

*The Jacksonville-Duval Area Planning Board is much more complex in this regard. In part the Jacksonville clearinghouse is a COG composed of representatives from Jacksonville-Duval as well as the surrounding counties. But essentially the Planning Board seems to function like a planning commission in an advisory relationship to the Jacksonville City Council. On a *de facto* basis, with regard to most clearinghouse issues, the City Council is the clearinghouse's policy board. Staff and policy members of the Planning Board indicate that they have made recommendations to the City Council which would be redistributive in effect. We are in no position to judge this. What is clear is that the city-county consolidation in Jacksonville has produced a governmental mechanism which may be on the way to redistributing resources rather than problems in the metropolitan area. One piece of evidence is the great willingness of the consolidated government of Jacksonville (as compared to previous local governments) to seek federal resources which can contribute to local resource redistribution.

the entire region to tap into the new tax base which would be generated by the airport and its surrounding industrial zone. A certain percentage of this new tax base would be distributed to all of the municipalities in the Metropolitan Council area.*

It is not now clear as to which proposals for redistribution, if any, will prevail in the Metropolitan Council's area. We are impressed with the sheer fact of its serious discussion when compared with the absence of such thinking in the other clearinghouses we have observed. The two most apparent variables which would appear to account for this difference are the authority which the State of Minnesota has invested in the council and the fact that council members are regionalists as opposed to representing individual governments.

In the remainder of this section we shall deal with other characteristics of COG decision making. Who influences whom? Who gets what? Does the COG make a difference? The analysis is of course telescoped by this introductory section on the character of COG decision making. If the behavior of COG policy makers is strongly influenced by the governments they represent then other variations become less important. Nevertheless, there are differences worth exploring apart from the obvious differences inhering in the structure of the Twin Cities area Metropolitan Council and the Jacksonville-Duval Area Planning Board.

Who Influences Whom?

We have continuously been impressed with the observation that COGs need to be seen as creatures of their staff. Given the marginal involvement of most of the COGs' policy people, it would be easy to predict a relatively powerful position for COG staff. We have generally found policy makers to be only superficially knowledgeable about the A-95 process, and even less so about the state of planning being done by the COG. We have also observed that COG policy people tend to be reactive to agendas which are largely determined by staff. The evidence for the COG as a

---

*(Ed. Note: Legislation pertaining to this objective was passed since the writing of this section. A four-page analysis of the new Minnesota law is available from the Metropolitan Council, Capitol Square Building, St. Paul, Minn. 55101.)

creature of its staff is very strong except as measured by the COG's output. In that respect the COG is the child of its policy structure. Its actions and inaction reflect the constraints of its local government membership, not the more regionally activist position of many COG staff members. In fact it might be useful to see the COG as reflecting a continuing and unequal struggle between policy members and staff. Each time that staff push for a priority scheme, or for the adoption of a position which could be harmful to a governmental member, the COG staff could be conceived of as being subversive to the organization. It is even likely that some of the enforced staff turnover that we have seen in COGs reflects a policy need to remind staff whose organizations the COGs are.

The question of influences, staff and otherwise, would be a much more important one if the COG often appeared to stimulate actions which could be attributed to the presence of the COG on the regional scene. It is the question that Erie, Kirlin and Rabinovitz pose when they write, "the problem, of course, is whether patterns of decision making, policy outputs, or impacts change significantly as a result of having new institutions."[5] In the case of the COG, the answer would appear that while COGs are potential arenas for new coalitions, the COG has not been powerful enough to overcome the primary allegiance of its members to their local governments. In the largest part, the new ground for decision making engendered by the COG produces the same results one can anticipate without a COG.

In that the COG is a structure which encourages new regionally oriented sources of influence, we are somewhat optimistic about its future. Despite the constraints imposed by being an organization of local governments, the COG is a clearly recognized regional organization. This identification does appear to provide sanction for the emergence of regional points of view. We have repeatedly used the notion of regionalist in describing the behavior of certain COG members. There is little question that the COG as a new regional structure facilitates a kind of regionally oriented behavior. If OMB and HUD sustain an interest in regional planning and evaluation, we think that the COG will become a more active arena for conflict between localists and regionalists.

While the COG as a structure generally gives rise to new points of view, the weakness of the agency has made it thus far a marginal influence upon the behavior which goes on inside of it. Membership behavior in the COG is almost always best explained by the members' local governmental affiliation. If OMB and HUD were to begin to negatively sanction COGs which did not sustain a regional plan and point of view in their evaluations, it would strengthen the hand of those in the COGs who are disposed to regionalism. So long as the key sources of federal support accept a very weak form of regionalism, there are no apparent rewards to the leaders within COGs who might use their weight to establish new regional points of view.

Who Gets What?

Throughout we have discounted the COGs as a force in determining who gets what. However, we would not discount its occasional use as a forum in negotiating the question. A most useful influence of the COGs has been a negative one: their unwillingness (or inability) to interfere with the special resource relationships that the federal government has with central cities.

While the most that can be said for the COGs to this point is that they have not interfered with the resource balance of the regions, the picture with regard to the Twin Cities area Metropolitan Council seems potentially very different.* The Metropolitan Council is considering the adoption of a policy favoring "locational equity"—that is that the individual citizen should be able to buy the same package of services, for the same tax price, throughout the metropolitan area. In effect, who gets what would become a policy decision to be made by a particular governmental entity, but once that decision is made it would not be affected by regional vagaries such as the location of an airport or a shopping center. Regional tax policies would be used to equalize a locality's capacity to furnish a certain level of services, once the locality had made the appropriate policy decision and agreed to tax itself at a rate commensurate with those services.

The thinking being done in the Metropolitan Council would not eliminate areal specialization in the Twin Cities area, but it would redistribute the gains from some of these

_____
*(See preceding Ed. Note.)

specializations. It would not eliminate the distinctions between the level of services in different areas, but it would seek to insure that those distinctions were a result of locally adopted policies, rather than the tax windfalls which accrue to an area because of specialized function. This might be as much equalization of benefits as the Metropolitan Council feels it could risk. But coupled with a program of federal aid to communities and individuals falling below certain national standards, it might resemble the redistribution of resources (as opposed to problems) that we described in a previous section.

Does COG Make a Difference?

We will not continue to labor the point that the Twin Cities area Metropolitan Council will make a difference, and has made a difference. In 1962 the Advisory Commission on Intergovernmental Relations noted that there cannot be equitable and adequate financing of services "unless the basic fact of noncoincidence of service areas and areas of tax jurisdiction for support of such services is clearly recognized and effectively met."[6] These conditions are not yet effectively met in the Twin Cities area but they appear to be clearly recognized by a governmental form with some capacity to do something about them. We have not found the COG to make this kind of difference in the other regions we have observed.*

We have based our recommendations for sustaining the COGs on facts other than their current incapacities with regard to redistribution. The problems of regionalism run beyond the problems of redistribution (although regional government is often posed as a solution to these problems).

Every COG we have observed has helped to create a sense of regional community. Interdependencies have been sharpened and an institution has been created which continuously poses expectations for regional action. The COG has had some small successes in an area of American governance where there has been very little public willingness to recognize the existence of problems.

COGs are becoming a recognizable force in the environment of regional single purpose agencies. The very existence

---

*Except possibly Jacksonville, whose uniqueness we have commented upon in a previous footnote on p. 70.

of the COG and the use of its A-95 power continuously pose questions of whether the region is advantaged by the growth of single purpose regional agencies.

Some COGs are cautiously beginning to experiment with the offering of regional services to and on behalf of their member governments. This service function will make a difference, just as effective single purpose service agencies have made a difference in the life of metropolitan areas. This willingness by some COGs to be of service coupled with the growth of single purpose agencies seems to have ignited interest in some states in the idea of regional multi-purpose agencies or in the evolution of the COG into an umbrella agency, where it would have major policy influence over the action of a variety of single purpose agencies.

The great difference the COG has made is in helping to create a regional community of interest around the formerly isolated actions of different local governments. It has been a relatively effective coordinator as a third party; as a cata-lyst in bringing adjoining governments to concern them-selves with their impact on each other's goals. It has been ineffective as the promulgator of a regional point of view with which others are helped (or forced) to coordinate.

In assessing whether the COG has made a difference we continue to ask that the COG be seen developmentally. The differences it has made as a new institution of government are real and important—but they are hardly commensurate with the regional tasks as we outlined them in the early part of this book. These tasks were to plan for those activities which were prerequisite to the jurisdictional crossings which reflect a region, to regulate effectively those actions where the action of one government is negated by the inaction of another, and to offer those services where scale dictates a regional base of operation. The COG which cannot make a difference with regard to these tasks ought not to survive, at least if that survival blocks the emergence of a regional governing force. The clearance function is important but it does not approximate the regional governing task. A federal expectation that the COG will be able to plan for regional development, and that it will use the A-95 process to seek the implementation of its plans, seems precisely the strain that can force the evolution of the COG or insure its termination. The fact that the COG has made a difference warrants its continued support—the inadequacy of the difference it has made, when measured by the regional governing task, demands that the heat be kept on the COG to plan and evaluate despite (and because) of the fact that its current structure doesn't permit it to cope very well with that heat.

NOTES

1 Steven Erie, John Kirlin and Francine Rabinovitz, *"Can Something Be Done? Lessons from the World of Metropolitan Institutional Reform,"* September 1970 (mimeographed) p. 18.
2 Ernest Inwood, "Some Economic Aspects of a Proposed Bay Area Metropolitan Transportation Agency," *Annals of Regional Science,* December 1969, p. 241.
3 Oliver Williams, Harold Herman, Charles Liebman and Thomas Dye, *Suburban Differences and Metropolitan Policies,* University of Pennsylvania Press, 1965, p. 301.
4 For an interesting development of some of these ideas on distribution, see Aaron Wildavsky, "The Empty Head Blues: Black Rebellion and White Reaction," *The Public Interest,* Spring 1968, pp. 3-16.
5 Erie, Kirlin and Rabinovitz, *op cit.,* p. 11.
6 Advisory Commission on Intergovernmental Relations, *Alternative Approaches to Governmental Reorganization in Metropolitan Areas,* Washington, D.C., June 1962, p. 8.

VI. DEVELOPMENTAL ISSUES FOR THE COG

We have posited a direction for the COGs—to achieve the capacity to deal with the problems of regional governance. Toward that end we recommend sustained federal pressure on the COGs to engage in regional planning and evaluation. But of course it is presumptuous to assume that the membership of the COGs desires that COGs attain a capacity to pursue these regional tasks. In discussing the developmental issues facing COGs, one needs first to get some agreement about the direction of the organization's objectives. On one level the COG is seen by its membership as a defensive device against state and federal intervention,* and at another level its actions seem little more than a ritual that local governments perform in order to insure their eligibility for federal funds.

If these are the real objectives of COG membership then the COGs' actions ought to be aimed at doing as little as possible about the issues of regional governance, while appearing to be sufficiently active to placate the relevant federal and state agencies. The history of some COGs might be seen as consistent with these tactics. We do not propose to treat the developmental issues facing the COG on these minimal terms nor on the basis of fulfilling the regional tasks we have posited. It seems more appropriate to suggest that the COGs' development should be seen in the light of the COG membership's willing acceptance of an instrumental role for the COG in achieving the goals of Section 204 of the Demonstration Cities and Metropolitan Development Act of 1966, the Intergovernmental Cooperation Act of 1968, and OMB's implementing circular for these two pieces of legislation. So long as the COG accepts an instrumental role with regard to A-95 it seems fair to sug-

---

*The Sacramento Regional Area Planning Commission in its regional planning statement noted, "any failure on the part of local government to actively respond to those issues of regional significance is an open invitation to federal and state agencies to intervene."[1]

gest developmental problems and directions deriving from this role. We also assume that the OMB would be interested in assisting COGs to develop so that they can implement Circular A-95.

From a developmental standpoint we are less interested in those A-95 objectives which call for the performance of clearinghouse functions. The COGs' problems are minor with regard to these functions. The key developmental problems for the COG derive from Section 204 of the Demonstration Cities and Metropolitan Development Act of 1966. The language in this section calls for a variety of projects to be submitted for review to "any area-wide agency which is designated to perform metropolitan or regional planning for the area within which the assistance is to be used, and which is, to the greatest practicable extent, composed of or responsible to the elected officials of a unit of area-wide government or the units of general local government within which jurisdictions such agency is authorized to engage in such planning. . . ." Section 204 then goes on to require that the COG review "shall include information concerning the extent to which the project [under review] is consistent with the comprehensive planning developed or in the process of development. . . ."[2]

As this report has continuously noted, the COG finds itself with a structure which seems unable to perform the kind of reviews required by Section 204 and implementing Circular A-95. If one accepts the effective implementation of the A-95 process as a major role for the COG, then the primary task for the COG is to complete its regional planning. This task is made more complex by the recent enlargement of A-95 coverage to include a variety of socially oriented programs. COGs must develop a whole new planning agenda or adopt the plans of other regional and governmental agencies unless the OMB and HUD are willing to continue to let COGs review proposed projects against nonexistent plans.

With the completion and adoption of its plans (or any portion of its plans) the COG must turn its attention to the issues of implementation. Its most available tool is the A-95 process, but that in a sense is after the fact. The COG must take steps to persuade its member governments to embrace the regional plan as a policy guide to local action. The COG must publicly deal with the failure of any local governments to adopt the regional plan, either by modifying COG regional plans or by using the A-95 process for negative sanctions against the local government. Inherent in the idea of regional interdependencies is the assumption that inaction by one unit compromises the action of other units of government. If regional planning is based on these interdependencies, then the mature COG must work to insure the likelihood of mutual action where necessary.

Thus the major developmental task for the COG is to complete the adoption of policy guidelines for regional action. Once this is done the COG, if it adheres to an A-95 process which includes planning/clearance/evaluation, is confronted with a whole new set of developmental tasks. Completed regional plans, if not adopted by local government or used as the basis for A-95 review, must induce trauma among COG staff, among HUD and OMB staff, and hopefully among COG policy makers.

This trauma could be expected to lead to a concern for a number of other issues affecting the development of the COG:

1. Does the COG have an adequate staff complement? Have the irregularities of federal funding, coupled with the fear by some local governments of hiring a competent COG staff, led to an inappropriate dependence upon consultant resources?

2. Does the COG have appropriate professional skills on its staff? Life in the COG would seem to call for staff with a strong political sense coupled with technical skills. The COG is not an innocent bearing truth to the political market place. COG staff must be prepared to handle conflict and on occasion to induce conflict as a tactic for helping to implement regional plans.

3. Does the COG's voting procedures and the composition of its membership work to insure ineffective action in implementing COG plans? In particular, would the addition of some membership on the COG which does not represent local government be of help? Regional planning commissions have long made use of nongovernmental representatives. The North Central Texas COG has a number of regional leaders on its board who do not represent local government. The Association of Bay Area Governments has recently changed its bylaws to allow its president and vice president to be independent of local government affiliation.

Does the COG make the best possible use of citizen participants in its internal decision processes as a way of introducing conflict and better sustaining a regional point of view? Theoretically, we are impressed with the likelihood that COG decision makers who do not represent local government would be better able to argue for a regional point of view. The issue deserves more careful study.

4. Would it be possible for the COG to develop a nongovernmental constituency in addition to its governmental members? This might be in the form of conservation groups, housing groups, etc., which saw the COG as a potentially effective device for achieving their own goals, and were prepared to ally themselves with the COG.

5. Should COGs seek less local budgetary support and more state support to be used in matching federal funds? Would such a move somewhat attenuate COG dependence upon local government? We are of course aware of the counter-suggestion that would make the COG totally dependent upon local membership fees. We think this would be the *coup de grace* to the COGs' regional planning capacities. If this were to happen we would predict that COG development would become arrested at the level of a clearing-house and regional plans would officially become a collation of local planning.

6. Should there be a change in the membership base of the COG? In too many instances we sense that the COG embraces an artificial number of jurisdictions. In particular these include the more rural counties which have been buckled into the COG for administrative neatness, but in fact are not an integral part of the metropolitan area. We have observed that these outlying units are less interested in regional planning and regional action, because in fact they share far less interdependence with the core members of the region. A smaller membership base for the COG might facilitate regional planning and remove from COG policy making those local governments which act to obstruct, because they ought not to have been on the COG in the first place.

In the following pages we will offer further detail on some of these developmental issues based upon our observations in the field.

Representation on COG

Victor Jones has emphasized that a most serious danger to COGs "is ideological warfare over the representation base of the governing body."[3] Field observation does not generally bear out this prediction. All COG leadership seems to agree that if their agencies do not now have a population-weighted voting scheme, they will shortly be moving in that direction. Undoubtedly a victory by the City of Cleveland in its lawsuit challenging its COG's constituent unit voting system will hasten the movement toward one man/one vote.

While the pattern of COG representation may be resolved by the combined influence of the Cleveland lawsuit and a changed sense of fair play, the developmental issues for the COG are extremely interesting. Ideologically, COG leadership continually makes the point that it is a coming together of governments—not a new level of government. Any move which places COG representation on a population base rather than a unit of government base challenges the COG as a council *of* governments.

If the large central city is the most obvious victim of unit-of-government voting schemes, in most cases it seems to be a willing victim. Three explanations come to mind, and they all appear to be useful in clarifying some of the COGs' continuing problems: (1) as one central city representative to a COG said, "the COG simply isn't important enough to get into a struggle over voting strength"; (2) the counterpart to this last comment is that central city leaders know that the COG is unwilling to risk taking action which might hurt the central city, and therefore voting becomes a formality not worth arguing over; (3) all local governments may be against a population-based voting scheme because it can increase the likelihood that the COG would evolve into a new level of government.

It is this last point pertaining to the evolution of the COG that compounds the issue of representation. The "ideological warfare" Professor Jones writes about appears to have less application to COGs than to what might follow the COGs. In the San Francisco Bay area, where the issue of regional home rule has surfaced a number of times, a major debate continues over the matter of representation. Will the home rule agency be controlled by representatives from existing local government or will the representatives be directly elected? (Some interesting current proposals for the San Francisco Bay area call for a two-house system, with one house being directly elected and the other based on unit of government representation—almost a regional replica of the United States Congress.)

In the Minneapolis-St. Paul area's Metropolitan Council the issue is no longer whether the council will be based on units of government. The state has preempted the issue by appointing the membership of the council based on State Senate districts. In contrast to the San Francisco Bay area (where local officials are against direct elections) we found public officials in the Minneapolis-St. Paul area interested in having members of the Metropolitan Council directly elected, with the hope that in this way the council would be "more responsive to local governments."

If the issue of representation draws its importance from what the COG might become, rather than what it is, the comment is equally applicable to racial issues in the metropolitan area. We have assumed it to be no accident that the first lawsuit challenging a unit-of-government voting scheme was initiated by a black-led central city administration against the white-dominated governments in the remainder of the region. The irony, as some have pointed out in the Cleveland situation, is that the price for winning might be losing. That is, that Cleveland's current voting strength of 6 percent in its COG would increase to 25 percent under a one man/one vote scheme, but with the added consequence that the 75 percent would be much more likely to find a community of interest against Cleveland.*

On its face the issue of representation would appear to be simple. The tremendous differences in population between the members of the COG would, as a matter of equity, appear to demand a weighted voting scheme. But the issue is quickly complicated by questions of what the COG is evolving into and the implication of this evolution for minority-majority relations. Local government officials are continuously wary of regional government which would compromise their authority (whatever is left after single purpose districts and special authorities) and minority

---

*There are some suggestions that the white-dominated governments in Cleveland's regional area have already discovered this "community of interest." A report in *City* magazine notes that the Northeast Ohio COG's "board members display the kind of vindictiveness and petty behavior that a growing number of suburban officials are showing toward the city."[4]

political leadership is equally wary. Many minority leaders will echo the comment of the director of Indianapolis's Urban League about the emergence of "Uni-gov." He has been quoted as saying, "I think that blacks envisioned that Indianapolis someday, like some other cities, possibly might evolve in the direction of a black candidate for mayor. This hope has been dashed now."[5]

It is likely that we have arrived at the point in most metropolitan areas where neither central city leadership nor the leadership of other governments in a region want a Uni-gov. At the same time they are confronted with parallel governments in the form of single purpose agencies, and the federal insistence on clearance and comprehensive planning. The issue of representation is the link and the strain between local wariness of regional governance, growing state interest in rational regional action and federal interest in clearance/comprehensive planning. We have no evidence that unit-of-government forms of representation, even when weighted according to population, can implement regional comprehensive planning or the kind of rational home rule in which states may be interested. But population-weighted voting, more so than constituent schemes, seems to raise new possibilities of conflict for local governments because it has too much kinship to the idea of a directly elected council. In the face of these strains we doubt that COGs can reach a stable resolution on representation unless the federal government drops its interest in comprehensive regional planning as a basis for A-95 evaluation, or unless the COGs evolve into a home rule mechanism with a portion (or all) of their members not representative of local government.

Citizen Participation

It is always difficult to determine whether talk of citizen participation in the COG is meant to compensate for the absence of elected officials from visible minorities, or whether its primary aim is to link the COG to some non-governmental constituency base. Perhaps the answer is both. Whatever the speculation, the facts are not encouraging. The National Service to Regional Councils reports that 60 percent of councils have "citizen types" on them, but HUD reports that only 30 percent of COG policy bodies have minority group members. It is apparent that the overwhelming number of citizen members on COG boards would be better described as white and middle class rather than being of a visible minority. The data is damning given the location of COGs in population centers where the minority poor typically comprise a large measure of the metropolitan problem. Perhaps HUD's requirements for the certification of area-wide planning organizations will radically alter the situation. These requirements note that "procedural matters [with regard to planning] should be structured to allow minority and low-income groups to significantly impact the decision process."[6] These 1970 HUD requirements are not its first expression of interest in regional citizen participation. Apparently HUD staff have been seriously constrained from implementing their own requirements with regard to the procedures and the composition of the COG. If HUD regulations establish a context for structuring the COG's policy board, nevertheless the basic decisions on representation and citizen involvement belong to the local COG.

We have little doubt that COGs ought to and will increase the number of minority members on their policy boards.* Whether they do so with elected minority officials, or with nongovernmental citizen representatives, will undoubtedly vary, just as current practice in this regard varies. There are numerous COGs which, as a matter of principle and without regard to implications for minority representation, wish to restrict their membership to representatives of local government. Given the increasing election of minority group members to central city government positions, it is likely that current schemes for enlarging the central city's representation on the COG would result in more minority participation.**

---

*One other observation in this regard is interesting. The minority group politician on the COG can be "unreliable." That is, he cannot be counted on to mute conflict and to protect his local government. In public forums his minority status can overwhelm his "role set" as a public official, and he can be "disruptive." Thus, in a COG seeking to avoid conflict, the minority official becomes potentially suspect.

**This is not necessarily so in that the COG can develop a weighted voting scheme to account for differences in population. Thus the vote of one delegate from the central city may count X times the vote of the representative from the smaller governments. The result is that membership on the COG is kept small, and the opportunity to include a fair portion of minority representation can be avoided.

We are less certain as to how COGs will handle the involvement of citizen groups so as "to significantly impact the decision process." We go back to an early observation that local governments did not join COGs to create problems for themselves; they joined because the COG promised to serve local government and to help it win federal funds. The establishment of citizen advisory groups not bound by the norms of "mutual turf protection" would be apt to create the very conflicts which local governments seek to avoid in the COG.

Given our interest in "straining" the current structure of the COG, we urge that HUD continue to insist on citizen participation. We are also fascinated with the possibility that special interest groups such as the National Committee Against Discrimination in Housing or environmental groups (because of COG's need to develop an environmental impact statement required by recent legislation) could become a party to the A-95 review process, and in that way create further tension in a system whose current blandness masks the real policy conflicts in every metropolitan area.

Planning vs. Services

The North Central Texas COG (NCT-COG) states that "it has been NCT-COG's announced objective to not only provide long-range regional planning, but also to provide a balanced program of high visibility services and action programs directed at immediate needs of local governments."[7] In fulfillment of these objectives the NCT-COG operates a nationally recognized police training academy, has conducted training for sanitary district personnel and is very much interested in the possibility of a joint purchasing program for local governments. The developmental question for the COG is whether a concern with services is compatible with the preparation of regional plans which the COG will seek to implement. The earlier quoted NCT-COG statement seems to take for granted that a service orientation and the conduct of regional planning are compatible functions within a single organization. The experience of the writer in the Community Action and Model Cities Programs (both of which aspire to do comprehensive planning) suggests that a focus on program action by the planning agency tends to drive out its ability to engage in central planning. In the case of the COG as a service agency, it can get so tied into its action constituency (local government) that it loses the capacity to develop plans which may adversely affect this constituency. But one can argue that the COG is already tied into this constituency—it is an integral part of it. Thus a COG's interest in performing regional-type services for its local government members could be seen as highly compatible with the current structure of the COG. Walter Scheiber, director of the Metropolitan Washington COG, captures this compatibility when he writes, "at the heart of a COG's success—or lack of it—lies the question of just how much it can do for its local governments."[8] We have no evidence that regional planning, which could run counter to local planning and policy, is perceived of as a service by local governments.

We are back to the persistent question of why the COG should be forced into a regional planning activity which is uncomfortable to the COG and may even possibly lead to its end. The best answer we can offer is that clearance and service are important and worth doing—but they do not approximate the task of regional governance. As a result we have consistently recommended that the COG be expected to clear/plan/evaluate with the hope that the resultant strain would help the COG evolve into a form more appropriate to dealing with the problems of the region.

There is another approach to the relationship of services to planning which needs to be carefully evaluated. This approach would suggest that because the furnishing of services is so compatible with the COG's current structure, and because services tend to have an "everybody wins" aspect about them, that COGs ought to pursue a service orientation to its members. Through the furnishing of services the COG can become organizationally more secure because of its public image of usefulness, and because of its enlarged budget and staff complement. The COG is then conceivably in a better position to bargain with its local governments for the implementation of regional plans. The COG has something to trade with, namely the value of its services. There may be some parallel in this model with the services (particularly water supply) that central cities were able to bargain with as they pursued the annexation of their smaller neighbors in the past.

We find the above model suggestive, but we do not have

86

much confidence in it. We believe that regional services and regional planning are quite incompatible inside the COG as it is currently structured.* The Twin Cities area Metropolitan Council's experience may be instructive. The Council has chosen to provide major regional services through a newly established sewer board, and in another instance through county government, while at the same time preserving its policy influence over the offered services, and emphasizing its continued interest in regional planning and implementation. Apparently, by design, the Metropolitan Council has separated services and planning.**

We do not envy the COG the development dilemma inherent in the issue of regional planning vs. services. If services are needed and the giving of services is consistent with what the COG membership expects of the organization, how will it be possible for the COG to resist—particularly when its leadership understands that regional planning and a policing of implementation are most apt to cause problems for the COG? We would predict an increasing focus on services, a growing sophistication about clearance procedures, and a diminution of interest in regional planning which will be implemented, unless the federal government is prepared to pull COGs toward different patterns of action.

COG as Broker vs. Decision Maker

In our field study we repeatedly heard reference to the "mystique" of the A-95 process. We think the mystique is the carefully nurtured illusion of the power of the COGs' charge to review and comment. It is the largely untested power of whether a negative comment by the COG will serve to block (or modify) federal granting action. We are convinced that so long as negative comments are far between, they will have increasing influence on federal action. Federal agencies will find themselves unable to say yes

---

*This incompatibility hardly bars an uneasy coexistence of services and planning within the COG. It may be another strain which contributes to the evolution of the COG.

**The "services" offered by the Metropolitan Council and NCT-COG are not comparable. Metro's services are to its region; NCT-COG's services are generally to governments in its region. However, we are not comparing services, but rather the organizational structure for delivering them.

87

when the COG has said no.* (Conversely, federal agencies will have much less difficulty saying no, when the COG has said yes, simply because yes is the COG's customary response.) The Twin Cities area Metropolitan Council aside, this capacity to say no with the possibility of the no being sustained by a federal agency is the only "authority" that the COGs we observed have. It is not very much when measured by the size of the regional task, and it is even less when measured by the seeming inability of the COG to use the power of that no. COGs, of course, potentially have the sizable amounts of authority which inhere in each of their governmental members. These governments could, by consensus, give that authority to the COG. The likelihood of that happening on any important issue is not worth the speculation.

The central issue confronting the COG is one of authority. Can it be authorized to make decisions which will be binding upon affected regional parties? Obviously the question of authority is important to the COG if it is serious about impacting its environment with a regional point of view. For example, the San Francisco Bay area COG does not delude itself on this issue of authority. In the publication of its general plan it lists a number of voluntary possibilities for implementing the plan but ends in a call for a "limited purpose multifunction home rule agency."[9] There may be other alternatives to this kind of home rule agency, but there is no alternative to the need for authority to make enforceable decisions if regional plans are to be implemented. The A-95 process is potentially a substitute for this kind of authority in a large number of regional actions where federal monies are involved. But by definition its coverage is limited to federal funds.** By practice the A-95 option is seriously diminished because of the unwillingness of the COG to use the A-95 process as an instrument in realizing a regionally developed plan or point of view.

---

*We have observed two situations where the COG made a negative review, the federal agency ignored the review, and the COG protested. In each case the federal agency subsequently agreed that it would be more sensitive to negative comments by the COG in the future, and would attempt to honor them.

**We have heard the director of a regional single purpose agency threaten to resort to his agency's bonding capacity rather than federal funds if the COG was not cooperative in the A-95 review process.

It must again be noted that a number of those involved with COGs claim that the greatest impact of the A-95 process on proposed regional actions lies in early information and negotiation. We have no doubt that such negotiation can bring proposed action more into line with regional planning or with the plans of a neighboring government. And there are undoubtedly many possibilities for getting local governments to change their action to better conform with regional plans, without having that change be costly to the local government. Nevertheless it seems to us that there is far more talk about these early negotiations than there is action. The image of these early negotiations seems all out of proportion to their reality.

Given the thinness of the COG's authority, it may cast about for a more adequate authority base by virtue of state action, or it may deny the need for authority. A COG which is a service agency has very different needs for authority than one which is attempting to implement a regional plan. And a COG which conceives of its role as that of a neutral broker in the clearinghouse process needs no authority at all. As one proponent of this point of view put it, "the COG must be a mediator between forces—not a force of its own."

We wish our observations had given us better clues as to the variables which stimulate an interest in regional governance. Things are not all of a piece in the different areas we observed. Some COGs will be perfectly content to perform the role of a neutral third-party broker between communities, while others will constantly talk of the question of regional home rule. We do not think that the Twin Cities area Metropolitan Council is destined to remain unique but it remains difficult to specify precisely the issues which would dispose other areas in that direction. Obviously the three factors which we described as underlying the need for regional governance are present in different degrees in different regions—and the political perception of their presence, which may be the more important factor, is different.

We offer the following summary of conditions which probably would be conducive to an interest in building a regional authority mechanism:

(a) The visibility of regional problems to influential members of the state legislature. Even physical proximity to the state capitol may be a factor (St. Paul—Metropolitan Council, Indianapolis—Unigov).

(b) A growing number of single purpose agencies of regional scope. This may be the most important factor. It indicates intensive interest by the state legislature in regional problems, and conduces toward a sense of helplessness on the part of local officials in the face of the "jungle" of regional agencies which are independent of local government.

(c) A previously active metropolitan mechanism which has been effective in surfacing regional-type problems, although not necessarily effective in dealing with them. To the contrary, a semblance of regional success through voluntary cooperative mechanisms might act to depress interest in a regional mechanism with authority.

(d) A metropolitan area which contains two or more dominant cities, as opposed to one where the area is characterized by a core city and a commuter shed. Two dominant cities in a single region seem to create a continuing series of issues between them which need the help of a third-party mechanism to resolve.

(e) A region having large nationally oriented type industries located in various parts of the region. Leadership from such industries seems to be much less patient with local governmental fragmentation.

(f) Relatively weak county government. This tends to create a void in governance beyond the individual city level. However, a strong county, whose boundaries approximate the metropolitan area may itself be the most powerful force seeking regional authority.

It is not clear as to how to handle the black, brown and white dimensions as an influence on this seeking of regional authority. There is some literature which suggests that the apparent greater interest in city-county consolidation in the South reflects a desire by white leadership to keep the central city in white political hands. However, more persuasive is the argument that the white-dominated suburban fringe seems content to be separated from the problems of the central city.[10] With the coming to power of minority political leadership in the central city, it would seem that a standoff in favor of metropolitan fragmentation and areal specialization was in the making. The major obstruction to this political equilibrium is reality; there are problems which demand a regional decision-making capacity. And in the face of a detente between the central city and suburbia, state governments will continue to create single purpose agencies, while the federal government looks anxiously at the COG and wonders what its utility is for regional problem solving.

Thus the developmental issue for the COG is not a matter of being able to choose whether it will be a service agent or a broker while it eschews the role of regional decision maker. If the COG continues to be unable to operate as a decision maker, then the authority to make decisions will remain dispersed over a growing number of single purpose agencies or the COG will evolve into (or be replaced by) a more authoritative home rule agency. The COG cannot choose to banish the authority question from regional affairs; it can only choose to avoid the question and therefore insure that its resolution will rest in other hands.

The Umbrella Concept as a Developmental Goal

If the COG chooses to confront the issue of authority then it must turn its attention to regional single purpose agencies. It is not as if the region were without the capacity for regional action; this capacity exists in single purpose agencies and it exists in state agencies having a regional base for action. If the issue of authority is to be addressed then the umbrella-type agency controlled by the COG is the least threatening response for local government. Through this umbrella, the actions of the single purpose agency can be made responsive to the policy direction of the COG. The COG can do this by winning the right to review and veto the budgets, the planning and the personnel actions of the single purpose agency. But with one major hitch: the COG can do none of this without the acquiescence of the state legislature.* The state legislature may be most unwilling to

---

*Except of course with regional agencies which are a product of direct federal funding action (e.g., economic development districts, multi-county community action agencies, etc.). With these agencies COGs are likely to become increasingly influential through the use of the A-95 process. However, these agencies have no regional authority beyond the program funds they control.

create a home-rule umbrella agency where policy is controlled by local governments. The legislature may argue that the creation of single purpose agencies resulted from the inability of local government (singly or in cooperation) to take on the regional governing task. Why give control of single purpose agency policy to precisely those local governments that the single purpose agency was meant to end-run?

If the state is unwilling to create an umbrella agency under the policy control of the COG (and we know of no state that appears to be willing to do so—regional government for the San Francisco Bay area has foundered on precisely this issue), there are other options. One is the creation of a mechanism similar to the Twin Cities Metropolitan Council which has umbrella authority over the planning of single purpose districts. The problem for the COG is that the Metropolitan Council model of an umbrella agency is not formally responsive to local government. The council is a creature of the state, with state-appointed policy members who may soon become directly elected.

Another option is for the state to create governmental consolidations, or to enable their creation through local referenda. In either case, if successful, it is not the COG which has policy control, but rather a newly elected government with an enlarged population base.

One other option, available to the COG, is to attempt to become a *de facto* umbrella agency through the use of the A-95 procedure. We have noted some hints of this happening in the greater likelihood for COGs to be tough in their A-95 reviews of federally supported regional planning agencies. We expect this kind of action to increase. But the A-95 process, which is not reinforced by state legislation bringing state-established regional single purpose agencies under the policy purview of the COG, is inadequate to the regional task. A number of these single purpose agencies make very little use of federal funds (because of tax or bonding capacities) and therefore would only minimally come under A-95 review. The A-95 process, even if aggressively used, is but a small step in the direction of umbrella-type policy control of single purpose agencies; the step cannot be completed without the specific action of the state legislature.

In addition to confronting the relatively autonomous regional actions of the single purpose agency, COGs must cope with a variety of state actions which are being carried out through regionally based boards and divisions of state departments. Those states which grow in their metropolitan activities will increasingly cross the path of local government. The COG may offer local government a more powerful device for dealing with regional manifestations of state action—they can hardly hope to control them. In some cases, of course, as with criminal justice planning, the state may seek to incorporate its regional actions into the COG, rather than building a new state administrative arm. The observed problems COGs have experienced with regional criminal justice planning may not support this as a future model of action.

The developmental issues for the COG with regard to an umbrella relationship to single purpose agencies may be the most critical of all. It is the continued growth of single purpose agencies and their disconnection from local government which may lead the COG to an interest in the umbrella concept. But ironically, it may find that the state legislature which has been instrumental in the creation of single purpose agencies is disinterested in turning them over to the policy control of a COG. Thus the COG's interest in the umbrella home rule concept, coupled with the state's unwillingness to move in that direction, may be precisely the combination of circumstances to lead to a regional multipurpose agency (e.g., Metropolitan Council) which is not responsive to the COG. This analysis would seem to suggest that as the COG evolves and is prepared to deal with the issues of regional governance, it must give way to another structural form. If true (the Twin Cities experience and the San Francisco Bay area problems with home rule conform to this analysis) then the developmental issues for the COG are most difficult.

Whichever path it chooses—to be aggressive or to remain bland—the COG is likely to give way to another structure for regional governance, one which is less dependent on local government and more likely to involve state appointees or directly elected officials at its policy level. But this development depends upon the urgency of the regional governing task and the perception of this urgency by the parties concerned. Our metropolitan areas have been pretty good at confounding those who have urged the need to act on problems of governmental capacity. Despite the seeming imperatives for action set forth in this analysis we will probably continue to be able to keep our actions far below the urgency of our regional problems. In that case, a COG which is not strained in the direction of a planning/evaluation function may be the perfect device to continue to buy time for regional inaction, and the continued growth of single purpose agencies.

NOTES

[1] Sacramento Regional Area Planning Commission, *Now to 1990*, August 1970, Sacramento, California, p. 39.

[2] Circular A-95, *op. cit.*, Attachment C.

[3] Victor Jones, "Metropolitan Detente: Is it Politically and Constitutionally Possible?," *George Washington Law Review*, May 1968, p. 742.

[4] "Cleveland," *City*, National Urban Coalition, February 1971, p. 44.

[5] "Indianapolis," *City*, National Urban Coalition, February 1970, p. 29.

[6] Department of Housing and Urban Development, Circular "MPD 6415.1A," *Areawide Planning Requirements*, July 31, 1970, p. 12.

[7] North Central Texas Council of Governments, *State of the Region Report*, 1969-70, p. 16.

[8] Walter Scheiber, "Evolution of a COG: Tackling the Tough Jobs," *Public Management*, January 1969.

[9] Association of Bay Area Governments, *Regional Plan 1970-1990*, July 30, 1970, Berkeley, California, pp. 28-29.

[10] "Atlanta," *City*, February 1971, p. 37.

VII. FUTURE PROSPECTS

Which Way State Government?

The state and federal governments are not necessarily complementary actors on the road to regionalism. A major theme of state action continues to be the creation of special purpose districts which run counter to the apparent federal effort to give local governmental councils influence over regional developments. Only in a very sophisticated, almost Machiavellian kind of way can the current state and federal actions be viewed as complementary; that is, that the continued creation of special purpose districts must increase the "pain level" for local government so that they plead with state legislatures for the establishment of some kind of regional umbrella agency, which would then be recognized by the federal government as the regional clearinghouse.*

In a review of recent legislative developments, Norman Beckman was impressed with the increasing tempo of state activity in regional affairs. He noted that "33 states [are] now active in supporting regional planning districts and associations of elected public officials from governments of metropolitan areas."[1] The Council of State Governments takes an even rosier view of the state's potential in the region. A council report notes: "the state is, in fact, an established regional form of government. It occupies a unique vantage point, broad enough to allow it to view developments within its boundaries as part of an interrelated system, yet close enough to enable it to treat urban regional problems individually and at first hand."[2] The actuality of state performance hardly matches the rhetoric, but there is no denying the potential. Within the context of the A-95 process as the most significant existing force for regional action, and HUD funds as the most important sup-

---

*In some sense this approximates the sequence of action in the Twin Cities area, except that the umbrella creation must at this time be viewed more as an arm of state than of local government.

port for regional organization, the state is everywhere the most important potential force for regional governance. In California it is the state legislature which is active in creating regional single purpose mechanisms, and which is also active in considering a form of regional home rule in the San Francisco Bay area. In Texas it is the state government that has been a crucial support of the COG and of the general value of regional planning. In Minnesota it is the state legislature which has created a Metropolitan Council, called by an analyst of its experience, "The most promising and innovative means yet to plan and govern major metropolises."[3] In the other three states we have visited (Washington, Illinois, and Florida) the state is an equally crucial force in the environment of the COG, if only in its potential.

We have no evidence which would indicate a dominant pattern of state action. There is no rush to emulate Oregon's Metropolitan Service District Act which permits the creation of a multipurpose regional agency having broad financing authority.[4] Nor is there any apparent rush to replicate Minnesota's Metropolitan Council model. But the multipurpose, multijurisdictional special services district and the umbrella agency are only two of the options available to state legislatures as they deal with issues of regionalism. Others include:

1. *A reassessment of the role of the county.* If part of our interest in the COG clearinghouse, as a vehicle for regional governance, resulted from the fact that it was "in place" in almost every metropolitan area, then the county warrants at least equal consideration. Murphy notes that "counties were established on an artificial basis. Unlike cities, they did not grow up as direct responses to local service needs. Rather, they were imposed from the state level upon geographic areas many years ago."[5] In those cases where a county embraces the SMSA, it could be reconceived as the second tier of government (or as the only tier of government) in the metropolitan area. The impediments to this kind of development are severe; in many cases the capacity of county government is conceived to be very weak and this weakness has been compounded by the extensive use of single purpose districts within counties. In addition, local political balances often find the core city (frequently Democratic) unwilling to see the enhancement of county government (frequently Republican). Despite

these cautions, we expect that a number of states will show interest in the concept of an "urban county" where county government receives home rule authority over a variety of functions, while other governmental activities remain the prerogative of cities or "urban service districts" within the reconstituted county government. We deal with the urban county idea in more detail later in this chapter.

2. *The regionalization of state bureaucracies.* This is a process that is well under way. In its simplest form it may represent the decentralization of a state office for the purpose of giving service. In other cases the decentralization is for the purposes of regulation or planning on a regional basis. An important distinction in state regionalization is the question of whether the decentralized body has certain authorities independent of the state central office. We have observed that where such independent regional authority exists, a regional policy board (advisory or decision making) is generally established. Thus the state agency can decentralize its operations in such a way that by delegating authority to a regional board, it creates *de facto* single purpose regional agencies. In some cases the relative independence of these regional boards, established by state agencies, causes great strain at the state level. That is, the state agency feels that its regional arm is not sufficiently responsive to state standards and planning, and perhaps overly responsive to the wishes of the area in which it operates (to the detriment of state standards). In other cases the state arm is not primarily responsive to state or local government, but more to the function it has been set up to deal with, and thus begins to act like a "true" special purpose district.

This description of different patterns of state agency regionalization suggests some models which might have broad applicability in determining which regional activities are best performed by the state, which by the region, and which by a special purpose agency in the region.

> (a) The regional operation which ought to be an integral part of state government: The activity which best fits this model ought to be one where tight adherence to state standards and planning is critical, and where it is most important that the function be tied into the performance of similar functions around the state and comparatively less important that it be responsive

to other actions within the region. Water quality control might be an example.

(b) The regional operation established by state government whose effectiveness requires comparative autonomy from state and local governments: Here the function would be peculiar to the region (or a particular region) with less emphasis on adherence to state standards (there may not be any) and emphasis on keeping certain decisions out of the hands of small inappropriate units of local government. In effect the protection of the function is most important, and the state is willing to incur a loss in coordination potential. The San Francisco Bay Conservation Development Commission, with its peculiar regional concern for protecting against bay fill, would be an example.

(c) The regional operation established by state government which is given a local policy board closely linked to local officials or forced to connect to regional planning: Here the coordination of the function with other regional functions is most crucial, so long as it operates within state and/or federal standards. A regional highway division office or an air pollution board could be examples. This kind of regional function is a likely candidate for policy direction by an umbrella-type agency if one is established by the state.

3. *The continued establishment of regional single purpose districts.* We noted this as the dominant state response, probably because it appears to be the easiest politically. However, we have speculated that the continued creation of single purpose districts, coupled with federal support of COGs/clearinghouses, creates an abrasive situation, with great potential for change. The anticipated result would be state willingness to create umbrella-type agencies, having policy purview over existing single purpose agencies, and a capacity to create new regional services under umbrella auspices. It is not at all clear whether these umbrella or multipurpose regional agencies, if created, will come under the policy control of locally elected officials, of new directly elected officials, of state appointees, or some combination of all of these. The churnings in California

around the issues of policy control of a regional home rule agency may reflect the fluidity of the issue. The California League of Cities strongly favors regional policy bodies that are controlled solely by locally elected public officials. Assemblyman John Knox, the sponsor of a home rule bill for the Bay Area, originally favored a directly elected board but is apparently willing to compromise on one balanced between locally elected officials and those who are directly elected to the regional board. The Los Angeles County Division of the League of California Cities in a 1970 study of "City Government and Regional Problems" also favors a board balanced between local officials and directly elected representatives.[6] San Francisco Supervisor Ronald Pelosi has offered the suggestion of a bicameral board with one house representing local government and the other composed of directly elected representatives.

The current national experience suggests that control by locally elected officials of new regional governing devices is the least promising option. As a result, the federal government may have to decide whether to ally itself with locally elected officials (as it is now doing with the COG) or with state efforts to create a capacity for regional governance separated from local government.

Throughout this report we have opted for a federal role which would support regional planning and the use of those plans in the A-95 review process. We think this federal insistence will so seriously strain the COG as to insure its evolution. At that point, the federal and state governments might finally find themselves in a complementary relationship where both are acting to support a capacity for regional governance which was something more than a council *of* governments.

We make no predictions, apart from an increase in state action with regard to regionalism, as to what specific actions the state will take. But there is no mistaking the growth of regionalism as an issue for state legislatures across the country. The reality of regional governing problems, the attractiveness of the single purpose agency as a means for dealing with these problems, the current dominance of the federal government as a supporter of regional governance, and the increasing visibility of new metropolitan governing options, all contribute to a volatile decision situation.

The Impact of New Federal Policies on Regionalism

Despite two pertinent pieces of federal legislation and the implementing A-95 circular, we remain unconvinced that the federal government has consciously opted to facilitate the emergence of a regional governing form. There is little question that the federal government wants something resembling regional planning; that it wants the opinion of the governments of a region in helping to rationalize local federal action; that it wants a capacity to render some services and to regulate some actions on a regional basis.* In effect, different elements in the federal government favor some or all of the ingredients which would lead toward regional governance, but there is no federal capacity to stand up and say that federal action will be taken so as to encourage state and local government to respond to the problems of the region with new governing forms. Given this inability of the federal government to take a position on regional governance *per se*, we expect an array of federal policies which will strain against each other, and which may settle for a clearinghouse which "clears" and gives service without being burdened by planning/evaluation. But a retreat to a services orientation is not the only policy option, and other federal policies may carry imperatives for regional governance which will continue to keep the federal government center stage on these issues. Based on our observations and analysis we see the following possibilities for federal action:

> 1. A continuation and a sharpening of the federal role as resource redistributor for the region. It is a role which Danielson also predicted when he wrote, "Federal aid increasingly will fill the gaps produced by the social irresponsibility of the metropolis." [7] Some have cautioned that revenue sharing, if adopted, would compromise this resource redistribution role by giving greater fiscal capacity to those governmental decision units least able to make redistributive decisions. We are optimistic that revenue sharing, even if adopted, can be conditioned by national standards

---

*This is somewhat like the story that Herbert Kramer of the Office of Economic Opportunity told about OEO's problems with the Congress. He suggested that the Congress liked the individual pieces of the OEO, but was upset each time it examined OEO as a whole.

to insure that the impact of federal resources continues to be redistributive.

2. We have continuously pressed in this book for a federal policy which would force the linkage of the clearance and planning/evaluation functions of the COG. It would require that HUD funds continue to be available in support of overall regional planning, and that the continuation of HUD support for the clearinghouse be based on evidence that the clearinghouse is using its planning as a context for the A-95 review process. When this is not the case we ask that HUD decertify the clearinghouse as an areawide planning organization and that OMB, in turn, decertify an agency as a clearinghouse if it does not have an overall planning capacity. This action would be consistent with the current language of the A-95 circular. Unfortunately, there is an equally great likelihood that HUD will seriously dilute its support of planning by the clearinghouse and that OMB in turn will settle for some clearance without planning/evaluation, as it is apparently doing at the present time. These kinds of policy choices by HUD and OMB would be in accord with their current assessment of COG weaknesses, but they would be disastrous in that they would arrest the development of the COG by letting it "off the hook" of the incompatibility of its current structure with its federally delegated tasks.

3. Another option would be for the federal government to say that it has done as much as can be expected of it in terms of furthering regional governance. The issue is then essentially one for the state to resolve, since in any evolution of the COG, the state is the policy "gatekeeper." This approach could be affirmed by making the state government the grantee for all 701 planning funds and giving the state the authority to recognize the legitimacy of a clearinghouse. There is a certain appealing logic to this kind of move. But in most states (not all by any means) it would also signal a termination of any COG development toward a regional governing mechanism. Most states would be unwilling to facilitate regional governance that was not based on local government, and would settle for COGs only as clearing agents. Or states would be constrained

by the aspirations of certain of their agencies to perform the regional governing task. As Harold Herman has noted, "state political leaders are subject to the same pressures that commit their local counterparts to continued metropolitan government fragmentation."[8] We think the state's interest in acting regionally is greatly increased by the independent action of the federal government on the regional scene. In coping with federal intervention the state can make major contributions to regional governance. But if the state controlled federal regional action through the control of 701 funds and the control of clearinghouse designations, a major current source of tension conducing toward regional governance could be removed.

4. In reviewing federal options we speculated that revenue sharing could be handled so as to preserve the redistributive character of federal funding. But what would be the impact of a sizeable amount of revenue sharing on the emerging patterns of regional governance? One way of avoiding the question is to conclude that revenue sharing would coexist with categorical grant programs, and the A-95 process (with its strains toward regional governance) would continue to be pertinent. But a revenue sharing program of great magnitude, whether totally free of "strings" or attached to broad functional labels, could radically alter (or eliminate) the role of the clearinghouse if the grants were made to the states. However, if revenue sharing grants were made directly to cities, or with a mandatory pass-through to cities, it seems reasonable to expect that there would be some kind of proviso that there be a clearance procedure for expenditures in metropolitan areas. At that point, the same problems would exist for a COG dealing with local expenditures of "shared" revenue as currently exist in the A-95 review process.

If revenue sharing for metropolitan expenditures was administered through the states, they could be expected to act, as many have done with criminal justice planning, by using regional mechanisms to help determine fund distribution. If the COG were this regional mechanism there would be reason to be concerned about a repeat of the regional problems in administering the Safe

Streets Act which has been detailed in an Urban Coalition report.[9]

The best that might happen with state administered revenue sharing funds would be a refinement of the model of state action described on pp. 97-8. According to this model the state would have to decide which functions are best administered by state agencies, which by single purpose regional agencies, which by a regional governmental mechanism, and which directly by the cities. The capacity of most states to make the above kinds of administrative delineations between functions is very much to be doubted. What would probably emerge would be some kind of politically acceptable formula for dividing new revenues between state and local arenas, followed by the use of a COG-type mechanism to divide local funds on the basis of population. Revenue sharing in the hands of most states would appear to offer little potential stimulus to regional governance. To the contrary, it might retard this development by removing the strains caused by a federal interest in regional clearance and planning/evaluation.

Unless the federal government should turn funding and sanctioning of clearinghouses over to states, there is little reason to doubt the continued importance of federal action with regard to regional governance. As noted above, federal importance on the regional scene could be attenuated by extensive revenue sharing (or by a great increase in block grants) with states. Barring either of these occurrences, we would recommend that federal policy governing federal regional activities be based on the following set of assumptions: (a) that there is an important series of tasks which demand a regional governing capacity, (b) that this capacity must include services *and* planning/evaluation, (c) that out of the strain induced by federal insistence on services and planning, a regional governing capacity will be helped into existence, and (d) that the state is the key actor in any such emergence.

Whatever federal funding pattern emerges (revenue sharing or categorical grant programs), it is crucial that there be federal standards which insure that federal funds in metropolitan areas would be spent primarily on the basis of problem incidence. Only in this way can we be sure that no matter what the structure of regional and state government, the superior capacity of the federal government to redistribute resources would not be undercut at the local level.*

The Role and Function of the Central City

No matter what the character of federal policy with regard to regionalism (or to revenue sharing) we have concluded that the federal government must develop and sustain standards which insure that federal assistance, wherever possible, contributes to the redistribution of resources in the metropolitan area. If this aspect of federal policy was made more specific and it was recognized and accepted by central city leadership, it might diminish their opposition to regional governance. With this kind of articulated federal policy, central city leadership could be reasonably certain that metropolitan government would not become a device to shift federal funds to areas of lesser need in the metropolitan area.

We are not aware of any projections which suggest that racial concentration in the central city will change significantly over the short (or even medium) pull. Given this fact, emerging minority leadership in the central city must be fearful that regional governing devices will dilute their resources and erode their political base. If we are to get regional governance with the agreement of, rather than over the opposition of, minority leadership, they must become convinced of at least four things: (1) that certain environmental and physical developmental needs can only be handled on an area-wide basis, (2) there is already a powerful array of governments in their metropolitan areas,

---

*We have previously speculated that in some instances a regional governing form might enhance the possibilities of regional redistribution by trading problems for resources. That is, the regional mechanism would dilute its concern with problem (or population) redistribution and replace it with an agreement that most resources would go to those in greatest need in the metropolitan area. No matter what the effectiveness or ineffectiveness of regional government with regard to redistribution we do not base our case for metropolitan governance on its greater capacities for redistribution. There is some evidence of such capacity in the Twin Cities area Metropolitan Council but we are hardly prepared to generalize from this. *Even with metropolitan government we would continue to insist that the best guarantor of redistribution lies in federal policy—not in trade-offs at any level of local government.*

104

in the form of single purpose agencies to which they have very little access, (3) that there are forms of metropolitan governance which are not built upon the corpse of the central city—they are two-tiered or umbrella, etc.—leaving the central city intact as a political base for minority leadership, and (4) that no matter what restructuring takes place, federal policy will insure that those in need in the central cities will have a priority call on federal funds.

The Regional Single Purpose Agency

There is probably nothing like the reality of governing a central city to convince minority leadership of the power of single purpose agencies. And one need not be too cynical to suggest that state legislatures may become even more enamored of the single purpose agency option when minority leadership controls the central city.

The real problems of governing the region will persist and new multijurisdictional regional governing forms will not come into being overnight. The political advantages of creating the single purpose agency, coupled with its seeming effectiveness when compared to other units of government, insure its continuity on the metropolitan scene. In addition, single purpose districts offer the chance to deal with particular problems without making changes in the structure of existing governments.

The single purpose agency is peculiarly suited for a problem-solving approach. Further, general purpose government does not lend itself to factions organized around problems. These factors make a continuation of the single purpose district likely and attractive. The growth of the regional single purpose agency also argues for an umbrella-type structure as the next important development in regional governance. The umbrella would have the authority (through control of budget, key personnel and planning) to see that the single purpose agencies act to maximize more general notions of well-being, while the identity and separate capacity of the single purpose agencies are retained. The object of the umbrella is to bring the policy of connected functions into a common decision framework, while preserving the advantages of functional specialization in smaller units of operation. We are impressed with the relevance of the umbrella model of metropolitan decision making to current issues in regional governance.

The Urban County

If historically the county is an administrative arm of state government, it seems reasonable to ask why state legislatures did not require the county (or counties in combination) to administer those functions which have instead been assigned to single purpose districts. The answer would appear to lie in two directions: the general administrative weakness of the county and its specific weakness vis-a-vis its major city.*

A 1971 *New York Times* survey of county government concludes that it is a rapidly strengthening locus of governmental capacity.[11] If this growth in strength is a fact, it promises two important developments: (1) that counties will increasingly come into conflict with single purpose districts, many of which were established because of assumed county weakness. We think that the likelihood of COGs "taking on" single purpose districts is increased when the county is a strong factor in the organizational makeup of the COG, and (2) that in a great number of metropolitan areas, where that area is embraced by a single county, the notion of an urban county as a single tier of government is the most likely step in the development of regional governance.** In addition to the urban county delivering a variety of municipal services to unincorporated areas of the county, it can perform those services and regulatory activities which are best done on a regional basis, while at the same time standing in an umbrella relationship to special districts within the county.

---

*This weakness is not always true. A major work in the field of regional governance studies the "Lakewood Plan" in Los Angeles County and comes to certain conclusions based on the real governmental competence of Los Angeles County to perform as an urban county. Unfortunately, it is a competence not yet often duplicated.[10]

**The notion of an urban county is often used to connote a single metropolitan government within current county boundaries, rather than the county as a second tier of government. In this report we use urban county to describe a second tier rather than a city-county consolidation. Interestingly, even much publicized consolidations such as Indianapolis-Marion and Jacksonville-Duval do not completely obliterate first levels of government. Marion County now has nine townships, and Jacksonville has four independent service districts with their own local governments in addition to the new consolidated government.

As previously noted, the state is the key source of authority with regard to enhancing the counties' functions. The caution, of course, is that in forming the urban county we may be institutionalizing a very short-lived governmental answer. Given the growth of our metropolitan areas, the urban county could soon find itself without governmental access to the new residential centers beyond its boundaries and to jurisdictional problems of the region.

If the urban county is a real option for regional governance, then the federal government must act accordingly, *if* it favors this development in metropolitan governance. It ought to recognize the metropolitan county as the clearinghouse without forcing it into association with adjoining rural counties for the sake of administrative neatness. Just as we have singled out the umbrella concept as having a good fit to the governing problems of multicounty areas, we are equally interested in the urban county as a second-tier government (and first tier in unincorporated areas). We think federal policy ought to contemplate both of these structures (the umbrella and the urban county) along with multipurpose special service and planning districts as appropriate governmental forms toward which clearinghouses should evolve. And federal policy ought to be used to further this evolution. Throughout this report we have indicated what such policies might be.

The Emergence of Metropolitan Government

A 1969 bill related to Bay Area home rule introduced into the California legislature by Assemblyman William Bagley makes the following strong case for regional governance:

> The legislature further finds and declares that although existing regional organizations have made significant accomplishments within their respective functional responsibilities, the continued proliferation of special districts presents serious drawbacks:
>
> 1. There is no overall political process by which scarce regional resources can be allocated among conflicting demands in a balanced and coordinated approach to area-wide governmental problems;

2. Regional problems must reach a "crisis" stage before agencies are authorized or created to attack them since there is no established pattern by which problems can be anticipated, planned for, and dealt with in an orderly fashion;

3. Special purpose agencies tend to separate functions which produce revenue from those which do not, again making a balanced approach to total needs more difficult;

4. Public interest in the operations of special purpose agencies is generally low and they remove functions from control by officials who are politically responsible and responsive to overall Bay area needs; and

5. The continued proliferation of special purpose agencies will diminish the importance of general purpose local government, reduce its vitality, and diminish its ability to attract the interest and support of its citizenry.[12]

The bill for Bay Area regional home rule did not pass but the issue is still very much alive in the California legislature. Baldinger, in his book on the Twin Cities area Metropolitan Council, notes that delegations from the Bay Area have been periodic visitors to study the Twin Cities area experience.[13] The point is that the governing problems of metropolitan areas are becoming better understood, and there seems the likelihood of new governing structures as a response to these regional problems. The continued creation of regional single purpose agencies is strong evidence that the cooperative arrangements by which jurisdictional problems have been met are increasingly recognized as ineffective. Nothing in our observations permits us to say that structural innovation is the way to deal with these problems in governance, or that any particular innovation is the best way to deal with them. To the contrary Joseph H. Lewis maintains that "coalitions . . . employ whatever governmental structural arrangements exist to further their aims. These coalitions will tend to prevent any change in structural arrangements that do occur from altering their balance of power over the distribution of costs and resources of interest to them. . . . Therefore, only if local coalitions . . . change can locally determined structural change in government be expected to cause significant change in cost and resource distribution."[14]

Lewis' argument would lead one to doubt that any locally developed structure would be effective as a force for redistribution. The COG as such a structure offers nothing to invalidate Lewis' point in our observation. Only the Twin Cities Area Metropolitan Council, as a new structure, offers some promise of effectiveness with regard to redistribution. And here it should be noted that the Metropolitan Council is not a locally created structure, but one created by the state. A comparative assessment of six COGs and the Metropolitan Council has led us to favor a federal policy of straining the current structure of the COG, with the hope that it might evolve into one better able (and with authority) to make governing decisions about metropolitan area problems.

Richard Hartman, director of the National Service to Regional Councils, has editorialized that "any challenges to regional councils are challenges to local governments."[15] At this time Hartman is right. But the implication of his comment is of concern. If we deny that there are problems in regional governance, then there is no point in challenging the COGs' effectiveness as a regional governing force. The challenge is immaterial. But if there are problems in regional governance, and the National Service to Regional Councils acknowledges that there are, then one ought to be able to see the regional councils as an instrument for regional governance and evaluate it in its instrumental capacity. A challenge to regional councils is then not a matter of challenge to local government, but rather concern about the effectiveness of an organization of local governments in meeting the problems of regional governance.

Neither the National Service to Regional Councils nor any other organization is expected to be suicidal through the use of self-evaluation. Generally it is the environment of an organization which commits "homicide" upon it. In this last part of the report we suggest to the National Service to Regional Councils and to the local members of COGs that the structure of the COG does not appear adequate to the tasks of regional governance. And this is only a challenge to local government *if they ignore its implications*. Local government is challenged and hurt if these regional tasks cannot be performed. The COGs that we observed cannot perform these tasks.* Local government does itself a disservice if it marries its interests in regional well-being to the well-being of the COG. By doing so it may insure that when state legislatures finally deal with the issue of metropolitan governance they will be less sensitive to the legitimate and important interests of local government.

There are potential forms for regional governance which preserve the existing integrity of local government. The umbrella or even the multipurpose services and planning districts could be such a form, particularly if their policy bodies were bicameral, with one wing composed of representatives of local government (perhaps weighted according to population). Or the urban county need not be a form which is threatening to municipalities, while at the same time aggressive counties would welcome it. The targets for regional governance are the single purpose districts which operate as independent baronies, and those functions which cannot be performed well enough through cooperative arrangements in a metropolitan area. *It is not a question of local government's competence; rather it is a matter of the inadequacy of the structure of local government to the task of regional governance.* The targets for restructuring do not have to be local governments. They may become that if local government defines its special interest as the protection of the current structure of the COG rather than how to deal effectively with the problems of regional governance.

In speculating about the future of metropolitan governance it is very easy to become the victim of one's own analysis. We are convinced (and have attempted to make the case) that there are tasks requiring a capacity for metropolitan governance, and we are equally convinced that the COG does not and cannot have this capacity. Given previous failures in the establishment of regional governing structures, the COG has been a major achievement—worth all of the effort and resources that the federal and local governments have put into it, *provided the COG is seen developmentally*, and not as a final form. Over the short pull the COG will continue to be worth the effort, provided that HUD and OMB have this developmental sense, and provided that they are not prepared to "rescue" the COG from

---

*The failures of the COG are readily acknowledged in private interviews by staff members and policy board members. Unfortunately, the public aura of COG achievement does not reflect these private assessments.

the strain it is experiencing and should continue to experience as a result of federal requirements.

All of the above seems to imply a sense of motion, of excitement, of development. But it is much easier to argue that the movement will be painfully slow and perhaps nonexistent. We will limp along as we have limped along because inaction still seems the least costly of options. Nevertheless, we remain optimistic, primarily because a clearinghouse exists in almost every one of our metropolitan areas where a short while ago there was nothing. And we are optimistic because state government is engaged with the problems of its regions, and because there is too much knowledge about the issues of regional governance in OMB and HUD to settle for the COG at its current level of development.

NOTES

[1] Norman Beckman, "Planning and Urban Development: Legislative Review 1968-69," *Journal of the American Institute of Planners*, September 1970, p. 351.

[2] The Council of State Governments, *State Responsibility in Urban Regional Development*, Chicago, 1962, p. xvi.

[3] Stanley Baldinger, *Planning and Governing the Metropolis*, Praeger, 1971, p. 215.

[4] Metropolitan Service District Law (1968), Chapter 268, *Oregon Revised Statutes*, 1968.

[5] Thomas Murphy, *Metropolitics and the Urban County*, Washington National Press, Washington, D.C., 1970, p. 2.

[6] Los Angeles County Division, League of California Cities, *Changing Role for Cities*, October 1970.

[7] Michael Danielson, *Metropolitan Politics*, Little, Brown & Co., Boston, 1966, p. 349.

[8] Harold Herman, "Limitations on State Action: The view from Albany," *Metropolitan Politics*, op. cit., p. 319.

[9] The Urban Coalition, *op. cit.*

[10] See Robert O. Warren, *Government in Metropolitan Regions*, Institute of Governmental Affairs, University of California at Davis, 1966, pp. 1-327.

[11] Carter B. Horsley, "Reform: a National Mood in County Governments," *The New York Times*, February 14, 1971, p. 1, 71.

[12] Assembly Bill No. 1846, *California Legislature*, April 7, 1969, p. 3.

[13] Baldinger, *op. cit.*, p. 236.

[14] Joseph H. Lewis, "The Effects of Power Distribution," (mimeographed), *The Urban Institute*, Washington, D.C., 1970.

[15] Richard Hartman, "Editorial," *Regional Review Quarterly*, National Service to Regional Councils, Washington, D.C., October 1970, p. 1.

VIII. CONCLUSIONS AND RECOMMENDATIONS

The sense of this report has been that the COG is not now capable, and must be severely strained and restructured if it is to become capable, of performing the necessary tasks of regional governance. It is a difficult, and in some ways unfair, conclusion to reach. The difficulty and unfairness lie in the fact that we have *imposed* criteria of effectiveness on the COG which would not be accepted by many of its local government members. Many of these members are not prepared to see the COG as a governing force, and would deny the need for any new governing structure in the metropolitan area. They would find support in Glendening's observation that "a new school of thought about metropolitan reorganization has emerged . . . called the 'realists,' [which] recognizes certain advantages in the fragmented metropolitan system and/or has developed a respect for the political difficulties, perhaps even impossibilities, of major governmental reorganization for most of our metropolitan areas."[1]

We are not of this "realist" school. We are less impressed with the advantages of the "fragmented metropolitan system" than we are with the possibilities of preserving a governmental pluralism *within* a structure which permits metropolitan decision making. In Jacksonville-Duval's consolidation and in the Twin Cities area Metropolitan Council we have seen new governmental structures which offer much promise. They are not an organizational "mirage," promising change and new capacity solely because of their structure.[2] They have generated a sense of excitement, they have coalesced new forces and surfaced new points of view, and they appear politically possible. They may yet turn out to be a "mirage of reorganization" (in Dale Marshall's words), but they are not that now.

The criteria which make us optimistic about Jacksonville's urban county and the Twin Cities area umbrella are the same criteria we have used to measure the COG, and

112

to find it wanting. These criteria are: (1) Can decisions be made which are supportive of the jurisdictional boundary crossings which people in metropolitan areas normally undertake in great numbers? (2) Can common metropolitan action be instituted in those areas where the inaction of one jurisdiction undercuts the action of another? (3) Can metropolitan action be undertaken in those areas where the high costs of duplication demand a metropolitan approach?

The COGs we have observed all have some real capacities with regard to each of the above criteria. The COG's planning staff see the problems of their areas as a whole, and they conceive of responses to these problems which are truly metropolitan in scope. COG staff are sensitive to the issues of scale, and to the interdependencies between functions and governments in a metropolitan area. We are impressed with the quality of thinking being carried out within the COGs we observed; many of our large cities would be well served if their planning staffs were of equal vision and competence.*

The combination of HUD's regional planning perspectives (and funds), OMB's A-95 process, a regional coming together of governments, and competent COG planning staff have all led to a metropolitan governing scene filled with new promise. The expectations of the COGs are very high—the delivery is, and may remain, inadequate. Within the COGs as currently structured this delivery must be limited to issues on which it is possible to attain consensus (or near consensus) of all of the involved local governments. The COGs can deal with problems of boundary crossings, the need for common action, or issues of scale only in those cases where all governments are advantaged by the action, or almost none are disadvantaged by it. We think there are significant areas of metropolitan decision making which lend themselves to a model of "everybody wins," or at least nobody loses. COGs interested in their survival would do well to explore such areas. But we would argue that the search for such areas would restrict COGs to "special element" activities of a primarily physical nature or to regional service giving (e.g., clearance of grants, joint purchasing, and training). The COGs would not be able

---

*There is the possibility that we could be wrong to generalize from the staff skills we observed in the six clearinghouses we visited. By design we selected from among the most mature and competent agencies (by reputation), and therefore the staff competence we observed may be atypical.

to use deliberately these special elements to further an articulated overall design of how regions ought to function—because the presentation of such designs immediately ends the game of "nobody loses," and with it the COG's ability to act.

Sporadic regional action through service giving and the occasional realization of special element planning is the essence of incrementalism—it is comparable to the actions of special purpose districts which dot our regional landscape. It may be all that American pluralism can tolerate in the way of centralized planning in the metropolitan area.

In making our recommendations, we proceed on a set of assumptions which moves us away from incrementalism and toward a centralized planning and decision-making capacity at the metropolitan level. In doing so, we will lay the groundwork for the evolution of the COG toward the umbrella or the urban county or the multipurpose metropolitan planning and services agency. But at this point in time the movement away from the COG *can only be on paper. In the here and now, the COG must be sustained.* The COG is not yet a block toward the development of a more effective metropolitan governing form. The presence of a COG-type mechanism in almost all of our metropolitan areas is precisely the reason why there is now hope and excitement on the metropolitan governing scene. COGs have helped to congeal a metropolitan community and to create a metropolitan point of view. COGs have assembled staff able to see solutions to problems across jurisdictional lines and they have given a platform to regional leadership. COGs have acted as a spur to state involvement in the region, and they have punctured the isolationism of single purpose agencies. We find the COG to be a mechanism worthy of (and reflective of) the intelligence invested in it by the OMB, HUD, local government officials and COG staff.

Had we wished to do so, this report could have been a glowing account of the many COG achievements. Instead the report was one which dealt in large part with the failures and the incapacities of the COGs as regional decision-making organizations. In this concluding chapter we underline the COG's achievements as well as failures, because *in combination* they validate a developmental strategy which would continue to use the COG as a primary vehicle in the pursuit of a regional governing capacity.

114

COGs have carved out a place for themselves because they have been useful, without being painful to member governments. They could continue to be supported by member governments, and by the federal government solely on the basis of their current utility as clearance/service-giving agencies. But to do so, and to ignore the requirements of the A-95 circular for a planning/evaluation function, would by leaving the COG in its current state make the COG into a hindrance toward the development of regional governance. *The core of our recommendations is that OMB and HUD must strain the COGs to perform in a way that it seems structurally unable to achieve, namely, to differentially evaluate the programs of its member governments based upon adopted regional plans.* We anticipate that this strain, coupled with the growth of regional single purpose agencies, and the increasing "visibility" to state legislatures of new regional governing responses, will lead to the evolution (or replacement) of the COG into a mechanism which can plan to deal with regional problems and implement those plans.

If sustaining COGs and straining them at the same time are central to our recommendations, they have led to a series of subordinate recommendations which are presented in the remainder of this chapter. To accomplish the straining of the COGs, both state and federal governments possess potent resources which are (or could be) crucial to the COGs, and therefore the leverage of each in "forcing" change in the COGs is comparatively great. But because this leverage is great, and because we recommend a policy which simultaneously seeks to sustain and strain the COG, we must caution against the precipitous use of this leverage. To push COGs too hard may insure their demise rather than evolution. Yet not to push hard enough may be to freeze them in a form which is useful to their members but obstructive to the development of a regional governing capacity.* It is a

_____
*In our willingness to use (and strengthen) the COG as an intermediate device, we find parallels in the following strong argument by Friesema: [There is a] "notion that any alteration of the status quo which does not amount to formal unification is nothing—or less than nothing. One manifestation of this 'all or nothing' orientation is for researchers to dismiss intermediate organizational change as only temporary expedients which prolong them before 'genuine' integration comes about. The argument is that special districts, contractual arrangements, etc., are used simply to solve immediate crisis problems and by relieving this pressure the status quo is preserved, the balkanized metropolitan political system still functions, and the day

delicate balance that state and federal policy must seek to maintain until there is enough will in state legislatures and in metropolitan areas to create more powerful regional governing mechanisms.

The subordinate recommendations for this "sustain and strain" strategy are outlined below in terms of the COGs themselves and the three principal sets of actors in their environment—federal, state and local governments.

Recommendations for the Federal Government

1. *Greater Coordination Between HUD and OMB.*

At this time there are two federal agencies whose actions are central to the well-being of the COGs: HUD because it controls institutional support and overall planning funds and OMB because it administers the A-95 process. As a first step we suggest that these two agencies hold a series of meetings to see if they can find common grounds for dealing with the COGs.* Given the increasing importance of DOT in providing basic planning support to COGs, it would seem wise to include DOT in these meetings.

The fundamentals of an agreement between HUD and OMB must acknowledge that the A-95 process means clearance as well as the evaluation of applications for federal funds within the context of adopted regional plans.

---

of reckoning is once more postponed. . . . In its metropolitan form, some would apparently rather see the system collapse so they could build from the ashes, than approve partial remedies, which by improving conditions keep the system operating."[3]

*A HUD reviewer of this material points out that such meetings have been held three times in recent years, "at the highest levels," each time without success. This HUD reviewer also suggests that the recommendations to HUD and OMB to sustain and strain the COGs are not real, because the "feds are the first to run for cover." We have already noted that federal actions are not a thing apart from local politics, and that there is strong interest in *not* straining the COGs. But we also believe there is a continuing growth in local concern about regional issues, and a growth in federal concern about the effectiveness of current regional policies, both of which may conduce to new tougher steps such as suggested in these recommendations. We too recognize that the most likely action is inaction but any worthy proposals could be faulted on that basis.

Once this is agreed to, the two agencies must determine a procedure for making the finding that a COG is not using and is not willing to use its adopted plans in the A-95 review process. When such an adverse finding is made, the agreed upon procedure must indicate how HUD and OMB, after giving the COG adequate warning, jointly go about cutting off federal financial support for the COG and lifting its designation as a clearinghouse.

We suggest that the above agreements be reached on a bilateral basis between HUD and OMB. After that, the two agencies, jointly, ought to involve all of the other agencies which award regional planning grants; as a minimum this ought to include DOT, EPA, HEW, Department of Commerce, OEO, DOL and the Department of Justice. A prime purpose of this involvement would be to secure agreement from these agencies that they would not support a COG with overall planning funds or institutional support if the COG had been disqualified as a clearinghouse and had its institutional support stopped by HUD.

A secondary purpose of coordination among agencies should be to secure agreement that a disqualified clearinghouse would not receive "special element" planning funds from any federal agencies. It also would be useful to seek agreement that all federal agencies would put their regional planning funds only into designated clearinghouses or into special purpose agencies which have an umbrella relationship to the clearinghouse. However, we are not optimistic about obtaining this difficult feature; it would be sufficient to get agreement that other federal agencies will not undercut the actions of OMB and HUD in lifting support from a clearinghouse.

2. *Additional Staff.*

If HUD and OMB were able to reaffirm that clearance and planning/evaluation are integral parts of the A-95 process, and agreed upon ground rules for decertifying COGs that are not prepared to recognize this integrity, they must determine how to staff this agreement. OMB has no field capacity, and is not likely to have one soon. Despite the great skill and dedication of OMB staff, they cannot continue to try and staff a national system of clearinghouses with a very small staff out of Washington.

HUD staff have been the backbone of COG support, and so long as HUD supports overall planning they will continue to be. But we suggest that each of the ten Federal Regional Councils employ a senior level person to work with clearinghouses, partially as agents of OMB policy. The problems of the clearinghouses with the A-95 process, particularly given the enlargement of the process to include many social programs, are the most natural agenda items for the Federal Regional Councils. COGs have the potential to develop an overall regional policy and can attempt to insure a federal response which will further that policy. This accords perfectly with the desire of the Federal Regional Councils to facilitate a consistent federal response to local planning.

3. *Improve Review Process.*

Even though the Federal Regional Council, in the field, is the most likely federal counterpart to the clearinghouse, it remains necessary to have an appointed liaison in each federal regional office whose grant programs are subject to A-95 review. It is simply unconscionable that almost two years after the issuance of Circular A-95 some grants continue to be processed without clearinghouse review, and without even awareness on the part of some "line" federal personnel that such review is necessary.

OMB must have a source in each federal field office that it can look to for help in securing that agency's cooperation in the A-95 process. Once this liaison is appointed, clearinghouses should be required to send copies of all of their negative A-95 comments to the Federal Regional Council, to the agency liaison and to OMB in Washington. The agency liaison in turn should be responsible for insuring that all negative A-95 comments are responded to.

In addition it ought to be his or her task to insure that a federal agency has a workable system by which the clearinghouse is notified of the federal action taken on each of the grants subject to clearinghouse review. Everyone in the federal government is aware of the terrible inadequacies of its information system. However, it is impossible for the outsider (including the COGs) to understand why it is so difficult for federal agencies to communicate their grant actions to interested parties.

4. *Clarify Clearinghouse Designations.*

If the above procedures (or something resembling them) can be agreed upon, they need to be communicated to clearinghouses and to affected local governments. In particular, the clearinghouse must know that it is expected to do overall planning, and to use this planning as part of the review process. And regional planning agencies must know that a collation of local plans does not constitute a regional plan, and will not be accepted as a context for A-95 reviews.

A clearinghouse which does not qualify for overall planning funds must, by virtue of the fact, be ineligible for clearinghouse designation. Just as HUD has given area-wide planning organizations deadline dates for the completion of certain special element planning, so must the clearinghouses be given deadlines for the adoption of overall planning guides for regional development.

HUD/OMB must make clear that clearinghouses will be decertified if they do not meet deadlines and if they do not use their plans in the A-95 process, once they are adopted. This decertification process, using appropriate deadline dates, could be tested with those older COGs which have already adopted plans and have systematically failed to make use of them.

5. *Setting Priorities.*

If HUD and OMB are interested in a sustain and strain strategy, they cannot ignore the specification of priority setting as a part of the regional planning process and as part of the A-95 review process. If the federal government is advantaged by a regional A-95 review and comment procedure, then surely it would be similarly advantaged by knowing the relative importance of grant applications in maximizing regional plans. The strain in setting priorities would be predictably great for the COGs, but this task would be equally difficult for the federal agency. A good locally developed priority system would narrow the decision latitude for the federal agency. Federal agencies need have no fear over the short pull, because COGs are not about to be able to handle a priority setting system. But federal insistence upon priority setting as part of regional planning could be a key point of leverage in furthering the evolution of the COGs.

119

If adopted, a locally developed priority system could work against the redistributive tendencies of federal grants. The best protection against this happening is to specify national priorities in advance of local review, and to indicate that local priorities which work contrary to federal standards will not be honored.

6. *Use of 701 Funds.*

We also recommend that HUD make clear that it will continue to administer 701 funds for clearinghouses directly, and not through the states. We think the development of regional governance is strongly abetted by having the federal government as an independent actor in the region. We would also be impressed with a process whereby the OMB sat down with the governors in each state and worked out a regional boundary system which had some coherence. As part of this agreement, OMB on behalf of all federal agencies and the governor on behalf of all state agencies ought to assure each other that these boundaries will only be violated (if at all) by mutual agreement in the face of overriding cause. In refashioning clearinghouse boundaries we would also recommend that the most rural counties be pulled out of the clearinghouse even though they are part of an SMSA. The more urban and interdependent the governments in the clearinghouse, the more likely they are to find the need for common action.

7. *Related Guidelines.*

We are impressed with the potentials of the Environmental Impact Statement (now required by law) in adding to the strength of the clearinghouse. The statement ought to become an intrinsic part of the A-95 review process, with strong consideration given to special interest group involvement in the development of these statements. In the same way, we would recommend that federal guidelines (perhaps based on Title VI of the Civil Rights Act) require the clearinghouse to append a "minority impact statement" to the A-95 process. This statement ought also to be developed with the involvement of appropriate special interest groups. Both of the aforementioned special interest groupings might help to constitute the nongovernmental constituency that we see as being useful to the COGs. Both could also contribute significantly to straining the COG in the direction of regional governance.

Recommendations for State Governments

Our recommendations in this area are necessarily slim because the focus of the report has been the federal government and metropolitan governance. But no movement toward new regional governing forms can make any sense until the position of the state is ascertained. The state is the one existing level of government whose jurisdiction includes the great majority of metropolitan areas. In the case of the COGs the state is an erratic but always potentially powerful part of their environment.

On the legislative policy level the state would appear to have two basic options available to it with regard to regional governance.

1. *Inaction coupled with single purpose agency creation.*

In this case, currently the dominant one, the state stays clear of its options with regard to the urban county concept or to multipurpose, multijurisdictional devices. In a sense, the state surrenders its initiatives on regionalism by continuing to create or enabling the creation of regional special purpose districts. But it is our conclusion that the continued creation of special purpose districts is itself a fact which insures that the state will at some point have to consider the possibility of new multipurpose, multijurisdictional forms.

2. *The multipurpose, multijurisdictional options.*

Under this option states might support umbrella agencies, multipurpose special service and planning districts or urban counties. Whether any of these forms are preferable or more appropriate would seem to depend on factors that vary from region to region such as geography, the strength of local government, and the "density" of single purpose activity on the metropolitan scene.

While state legislative action is the long-term key to regional governing capacity, there is a body of *ad hoc* regional policy being developed now by major state agencies. We are impressed with the tendency of aggressive state

121

agencies to make their presence felt in regional affairs. We recommend that the pattern of state regionalization be determined on the basis of function, rather than factors peculiar to the leadership and "muscle" of different state departments. We suggest three basic patterns for state agency regionalization:

> 1. Decentralization of services/planning/regulation to the region, with bureaucratic lines indicating the tightest connection to the state level for purposes of policy and program standards.
>
> 2. Decentralization of services/planning/regulation and policy making to the region, with the insistence that this policy making be tied into a regional planning or umbrella mechanism as well as to state standards.
>
> 3. Decentralization of authority and service/regulation to the region with no specification for connection to state or to a regional mechanism— in effect the "true" single purpose agency.

For further details on these recommendations see pages 95-99.

Recommendations for Local Government

1. *Meet Qualifications.*

The central city administration must organize itself to take advantage of the A-95 clearance procedures so that it can develop more influence over all of the governmental and nongovernmental action, using federal funds, which takes place in the central city. In effect, the central city must use the A-95 procedure as an entrée for rationalizing all federally supported action to insure that it is supportive of the aims of local general purpose government.

2. *Maintain Direct Access to Federal Funding.*

Central city leadership must recognize that there are two-tiered forms of regional governance which sustain the central city's political integrity. It is these two-tiered forms which offer the greatest likelihood of the central city retaining its special funding relationships to the federal government. We recommend that the central city fight to preserve its federal relationships, no matter what the form of regional governance, because they offer the best guarantee for resource distributions to those with the greatest need.

3. *Increase Minority Participation.*

The political leadership of minority communities must begin to invest more of their time in matters of regional governance. The willingness of this leadership to accept new regional governing forms may be increased if they are convinced that:

> (a) certain needs can only be handled on an area-wide basis;
> (b) there is already a powerful array of governments in the region through single purpose agencies;
> (c) there are forms of metropolitan government which are not built on the corpse of the central city;
> (d) and if they are assured that federal resources will continue to be redistributive in character no matter what the form of regional governance.

4. *Clarify Autonomy.*

Local government must separate itself conceptually from the COGs. An attack upon the effectiveness of the COGs must not be interpreted as an attack upon local government. The COG is only an *instrument* of local government; the COG may not be effective in dealing with regional issues, and local government ought to be prepared to look at new regional forms which may be more effective.

5. *Relationship to Urban County.*

Where the domain of county government approximates the metropolitan area, the urban county can be a very useful and likely next step, if the county conceives of itself as a second-tier mechanism rather than a consolidation of the municipalities within the county into a single government. Our conception of the urban county is one which would function like an umbrella, having policy control over all single purpose agencies in the county, and a veto over all local planning which has important multijurisdictional implications. We have urged that where metropolitan

123

geography permits, the more rural counties be removed from the COG, so that a single county and its cities constitute COG membership. In this way the chance for the county to evolve into a "true" second-tier mechanism would be greatly increased.

Recommendations for the COGs Themselves

We have attempted to make our recommendations consistent with our argument that a more potent regional governing structure than the COG is needed, and that a federal strategy of sustaining and straining the COGs would be most likely to move them in the direction of becoming stronger. In this section, it would be gratuitous for us to make recommendations to the COGs, where the intended result was to contribute to the COGs' organization problems. Instead our recommendations are differentially addressed to two different constructs of the COG: one with a primary services orientation and one which is primarily oriented to regional planning/implementation.*

1. *The Services-Oriented COG.*

This type of COG should seek to neutralize federal pressures which look to the COG to use its planning as a context for the A-95 review and want the COG to include priority setting as a part of regional planning. The services-oriented COG should be most interested in regional planning which is a collation of local plans, or in regional plans which are couched in the broadest generalizations. This COG should tend to resist citizen participation as well as the building of a nongovernmental constituency external to the COG.

A constituent unit form of representation on the COG's policy board would seem most appropriate to its services-orientation. The *authority* to make regional decisions need not be an issue for this COG—it is a catalyst, a mediator, a force for communication, but not an agent with an independent point of view on regional issues. This COG should seek to be the regional clearance agent par excellence. The services COG should offer technical assist-

*Empirically, all COGs seem to be somewhat oriented in both directions—planning and services, but it is the primary tendency, in either direction, that is most useful for developing recommendations.

124

ance to its member governments and serve as an aggressive source of information about federal grants. The best of these COGs can become highly skilled in discovering the grounds for common action between local governments, and facilitating these common actions through cooperative arrangements between governments or by offering such action through the COG organization.

We have made the point that the most competent of these services-oriented COGs will fill a major need on the regional scene. They will be worthy of federal support, and they will make an important contribution to regional well-being. They may be the best we can hope for, and in that case it could be a serious error for OMB and HUD to strain the services-oriented COGs by requiring them to perform acts which their structure cannot tolerate.

The foregoing is a highly optimistic projection of the potentials of the services-oriented COG. Even if these potentials were capable of realization they would not be commensurate with the tasks of regional governance. Rather this type of COG would be likely to become a block to further development of more adequate regional governing forms. Because of the utility of the services-oriented COGs we would sustain them, but we would also strain them because of the gap between what they are and what they need to be.

2. *The Planning/Implementation-Oriented COG.*

The policy and professional leadership of this type of COG must be prepared to enter into a covert alliance with HUD and OMB and welcome the heat and the strain that these federal agencies can supply. In the face of this strain there will be the constant opportunity for the regionalist position in the COG to surface, and for regionally oriented leadership to seek assistance from the state legislature in improving the COGs' ability to deal with their regional planning/implementation tasks.*

We also recommend the following actions to the planning/implementation-oriented COG, many of which are the obverse of the recommendations made to the services-oriented COG: The leadership of this COG needs to be able

---

*We have cited the experience of the Association of Bay Area Governments in calling for legislation which would establish a "limited function, multipurpose regional government."

to risk making distinctions between member governments. And it needs, as a matter of course, to include priorities for action as part of its regional planning. While it is a Council *of* Governments—it nevertheless tries to be a thing apart; a force for *regional* planning and action. It should be moving toward a population-weighted voting system, as well as the involvement of citizen participants and nongovernmental constituency groups in the decision making of the agency.

This planning/implementation COG needs to see the A-95 process as its best current opportunity for the realization of its regional plans. It needs constantly to attempt negative A-95 evaluations, and it needs to be abrasive continuously with federal agencies which ignore these evaluations. This COG needs to set itself as the central agency for regional policy-making, and the likeliest objects of its concern are federally supported regional planning agencies and state-created single purpose districts. It ought to try to use the A-95 process to gain *de facto* control over the policy-making of federally supported regional agencies (e.g., economic development districts, comprehensive health planning agencies, multicounty community action agencies, etc.), and where possible over state-created, single purpose agencies which use federal funds. It ought to be the sponsor of state legislation which seeks to place the COGs in an umbrella relationship with other regional agencies.

Can any COG achieve all of the above? We doubt it. But it can try, and in the process of trying it can establish local government as a primary actor with regard to the issues of regionalism. The COG may not remain as the vehicle for the next step in regional governance, but the members of the COG will be highly influential in determining what those next steps will be. To paraphrase a previous comment: the COG cannot choose to *banish* the question of governance from regional affairs; it can only choose to *avoid* the question and therefore insure that its resolution will rest in other hands.

*   *   *

We opt for a COG that engages itself with the issues of regional governance—and we opt for a federal role which makes this engagement the COG's only option if it wants federal support as a clearinghouse and regional planner.

We have no doubt that there will be many forces constraining in other directions. Some federal agencies and their local counterparts are not about to diminish the autonomy of their special relationships to each other in the name of regional well-being. And there are those in HUD and OMB who would be wary of administering regional planning grants and the A-95 procedure in such a way as to force the making of periodic findings as to COG/clearinghouse effectiveness. The mythology about the federal bureaucracy aside, it really does not enjoy the role of sitting in judgment on local grantees. But it can do this when an administration and the Congress become convinced that such action is less costly than inaction. We think that the issues of regionalism have reached that point.

The constraints at the local level are equally great. Both suburbia and minority political leadership would like to avoid the pulls toward regional decision making. But much as both parties may wish, we cannot avoid our interdependencies in metropolitan areas. The COG/clearinghouse represents a potentially important mechanism for dealing with these interdependencies. We recommend that these mechanisms become shapers of events in their region, not just creatures of them. We think the role of "shaper" is most compatible with the COG policy, leadership and staff that we have observed. To this leadership we strongly recommend the planning/implementation model of a COG.

NOTES

[1] Parris Glendening, *The Federal Role in Regional Planning Councils: Trends and Implications*, Department of Government and Politics, University of Maryland, April 1970 (mimeographed), p. 2.
[2] See Dale Marshall, *Metropolitan Government: Views of Minorities*, Resources for the Future, Washington, D.C., September 1970, p. 34.
[3] H. Paul Friesema, "The Metropolis and the Maze of Local Government," *New Urbanization*, Greer, McElrath, Minar and Orleans (eds.).

Other publications of
The Urban Institute include:

Community Control: The Black Demand for Participation in Large American Cities

by ALAN A. ALTSHULER

This volume presents the demands for greater participation being advanced by the black communities of America's major cities. It aims to elucidate the most pressing ideological issues, to sketch their relations to international currents and their roots in American history, to examine the proposals made for responding, and to suggest priorities for future research.

1970, 238 pp, LC 72-110439, Pegasus,
New York, paper, $2.75   *UI-7-107-6*

The Struggle to Bring Technology to Cities

This report describes barriers that prevent cities from using new technology for providing municipal services. Two success stories in overcoming these barriers—in Scottsdale, Arizona and New York City—are described as a basis for anticipating that better services could be provided at substantial national savings. A suggested strategy for making better use of modern technology includes (1) creating an urban applied research center for developing prototypes and to serve as a "consumers union" for cities, (2) aggregating the urban market so industries will find it more profitable to undertake development tasks, and (3) generating a climate of innovation to make city officials more aware of the payoffs of modernization.

1971, 80 pp, $1.95   *UI-68-108-73*

Blacks and Whites: An Experiment in Racial Indicators

by MICHAEL J. FLAX

Indicators depicting white and black status over the past decade are presented for 16 social and economic aspects of life, relating to income, education, health, housing, family conditions and employment. For each aspect, the data show relative rates of change during 1960-68, the size of the gap between white and black performance, and whether this gap has narrowed or widened from 1960 to 1968. For ten of these 16 aspects of life, *different* conclusions as to the progress of blacks are reached, depending on whether one makes comparisons regarding rates of change or the size of the black/white gap. Further insights into the meaning of these recent data are provided by assuming that black rates of change remain at their 1960-68 rate, and projecting the data to see when, if ever, blacks would catch up to where the whites were in *1968*. Further analysis of the data helps show why people may reach seemingly contradictory findings when evaluating data by only a single criteria. Tables designed to highlight comparative black and white levels and changes for numerous other aspects of life are presented. There is also a discussion of how recent research findings can help explain the interrelationships between black income and many of the other indicators.

1971, 79 pp, $1.50   *UI-85-136-5*

Other Institute publications

by Melvin Mogulof include:

Federal Regional Councils: Their Current Experience and Recommendations for Further Development

Federal Regional Councils were set up to identify conflicts in agency policies and programs, to coordinate agency actions, and to assign and monitor necessary action within agencies. This early evaluation of the councils for the Bureau of the Budget (now the Office of Management and Budget) concluded that the councils are a thriving new development serving necessary purposes, but are so structured that they fall short of expectations. Recommendations for improving the councils are included.

1970, 167 pp, $3.00   *UI-138-7*

Citizen Participation: A Review and Commentary on Federal Policies and Practices

This analysis describes the federal policies that have affected citizen participation and draws conclusions as to what impacts these policies might have on the forms and content of participation. Implications for future policy direction are drawn.

1969, 122 pp, $3.00   *UI-102-1*

Citizen Participation: The Local Perspective

This study, a follow-on to 102-1 (above), provides local perspectives on the subject. It examines seven city and county-based agencies to determine the effect of local conditions on the federal citizen participation policies as actually administered by different federal bureaucracies.

1970, 188 pp, $3.00   *UI-138-5*

The Urban Institute is a nonprofit research organization established in 1968 to study problems of the nation's urban communities. Independent and nonpartisan, the Institute responds to current needs for disinterested analyses and basic information and attempts to facilitate the application of this knowledge. As part of this effort, it cooperates with federal agencies, states, cities, associations of public officials, the academic community and other sectors of the general public.

The Institute's research findings and a broad range of interpretive viewpoints are published as an educational service. Conclusions expressed in Institute papers are those of the authors and do not necessarily reflect the views of other staff members, officers or directors of the Institute, or of organizations which provide funds toward support of Institute studies.

These research findings are made available in three series of publications: reports, papers and reprints. A current publications list is available on request.

DISCHARGED

JAN 3 0 1976
DISCHARGED

RESERVE

RESERVE
DISCHARGED

JS
422
.M64

245693

UNIVERSITY OF WISCONSIN
LIBRARY
Stevens Point, Wisconsin

DEMCO